Lizzie's Legacy

Lizzie's Legacy

More Quilts from a Pioneer Woman's Journal

By Betsy Chutchian

Editor: Jenifer Dick
Designer: Brian Grubb
Photography: Aaron T. Leimkuehler
Illustration: Lon Eric Craven
Technical Editor: Christina DeArmond
Production Assistance: Jo Ann Groves

Published by:
Kansas City Star Books
1729 Grand Blvd.
Kansas City, Missouri, USA 64108

First edition, first printing
ISBN: 978-1-61169-084-2

Library of Congress Control Number: 2012956507

Printed in the United States of America by Walsworth
Publishing Co., Marceline, MO

To order copies, call StarInfo at **(816) 234-4242**
and say "Books."

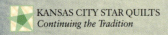

KANSAS CITY STAR QUILTS
Continuing the Tradition

PickleDish.com
www.PickleDish.com

Lizzie's Legacy

More Quilts from a Pioneer Woman's Journal

BY BETSY CHUTCHIAN

Dedication

**In loving memory of my father,
Neville Max Reed**
June 12, 1919 - May 10, 2012

*Thank you, Daddy, for all you taught me,
the questions you answered and the
mysteries you solved. I miss you every day.*

Acknowledgements

Many hands and quite a few shoulders supported me during the quiltmaking and writing of this beautiful book. So, I have many wonderful people to thank.

First of all, I want to most sincerely thank Doug Weaver and Diane McLendon who, without hesitation, permitted me to postpone this book when my father passed away. Without their understanding and support, this book would not have been completed.

Secondly, a sincere thank you to Jenifer Dick, my editor, for whose patience with my timing issues and writing blocks is so appreciated.

To Aaron Leimkuehler, my photographer, for your beautiful photographs and to Brian Grubb, my designer, for combining Aaron's photographs, the journals and patterns to make my book wonderful with your creative touch.

To Eric Craven for your illustrations, to Christina DeArmond for checking the math, and to Jo Ann Groves for all you do to aid in production, I thank you all!

To those who held me up when I fell down – my stitch group. You are such dear friends. You cut the pieces for *Remembrance*, sewed four patches for *The Lounge Quilt*, made blocks for *Friendship Baskets* and sewed some bindings. There are not enough words to express my heartfelt gratitude for your friendship – Betty Edgell, Sonja Kraus, Carol Staehle, Julia Berggren, Ann Jernigan, Pat Boyle and Marilyn Mowry. Thanks again to Betty for making the Honey Bee Pincushion, and thank you Renita Hall, for being a good listener and friend.

To Jo Morton, for your friendship and ever sympathetic ear, and to all friends involved in the pinwheel exchange that became *A Quilt for the Help,* thank you: Jo, Betty, Sonja, Carol, Julia, Ann, Marilyn, Mary Freeman, Annette Plog, Sheri Mecom and Deb Otto.

To my club members who were patient with me when I didn't want to sew and listened to me and gave me hugs, I thank you one and all.

To Pat Prestridge, thank you for sharing the antique *Brown Goose* quilt for inspiration and photography, and your friendship.

To Sheri Mecom for your lovely quilting, I so appreciate your talent.

To the members of the Carpenter family who gave Lizzie's journals to the Plano Public Library for their preservation in the Texana Collection, Geneology, Local History, Texana and Archives Division of the Plano Public Library system, Plano, Texas, thank you for preserving our family history.

To my son, Matthew, for help with typing the patterns, I thank you so, so much. And, to my daughter, Rachel, thank you for your support.

To Lizzie, Elizabeth Ann Mathews Carpenter, whose daily record of life has inspired me beyond words, thank you for taking the time to write in your journal.

And finally to Steve, thank you for your patience and understanding and for traveling this long and winding road with me.

About the Author

Betsy Chutchian developed a passionate interest in fabric, quilts, sewing and history as a child. Learning to sew on her grandmothers' treadle sewing machines and her Aunt Sissy's 1940s Singer paved the way to quiltmaking. While lounging atop a quilt on hot summer Sundays at her grandmother's house in Frisco, Texas, her mom would come by and point to the many fabrics of the 1930's scrap quilt and say, "that was my dress, and that was Sissy's and this one was Mother's apron" and so forth. There in those quilts were pieced so many memories, stitched with love to warm and comfort the family.

Betsy's interest in studying history began as a child with reading the Carpenter family record, a booklet assembled for the 1952 family reunion celebrating 100 years in Texas in which excerpts were printed from the journals of Elizabeth Mathews Carpenter. After graduation from the University of Texas at Arlington in 1980, Betsy received an antique quilt top made by her paternal great grandmother and great aunt and taught herself to quilt. It was then that the love of fabric and history united in a never ending pursuit.

About the Photography

The photographs for *Lizzie's Legacy* were shot at Missouri Town 1855, Jackson County Parks and Recreation, Blue Springs, Missouri.

Betsy began teaching quiltmaking in 1990 and continues to enjoy teaching and sharing her passion for 19th Century reproduction quilts with the club she leads at Lone Star House of Quilts in Arlington, Texas, and as she travels presenting programs and workshops across Texas and beyond.

Betsy's first book with The Kansas City Star was *Gone to Texas: Quilts from a Pioneer Woman's Journal* and is co-author of *History Repeated: Block Exchange Quilts by the 19th Century Patchwork Divas.* Betsy is co-founder of the 19th Century Patchwork Divas who have had quilt exhibits of their work in 2004 and 2008 in Houston at the International Quilt Festival. The 2008 exhibit traveled to Chicago, Pittsburgh and Long Beach, California. The group also exhibited quilts at the Rocky Mountain Quilt Museum in Golden, Colorado, in 2009.

In addition to quiltmaking, Betsy's passion for fabric has led to fabric design. Her first fabric line debuted in 2010 and the fourth in 2012 with Blue Hill Fabrics.

Betsy lives in Grand Prairie, Texas, with her husband, Steve, of 36 years and their 3 cats, Winston, Molly and Hudson.

Lizzie's Legacy

Lizzie's Legacy

INTRODUCTION

Robert Carpenter and Elizabeth (Lizzie) Mathews were born and raised in Kentucky, married in 1851 and in 1852 put a sign on their door reading "Gone to Texas." It wasn't until 1857 that Lizzie began writing, keeping a record of her work in which daily recordings of domestic life, the demands of caring for family, crops and stock all were noted in the journals as if she were talking to a dear friend. Together Robert and Lizzie, my great-great-grandparents, would have seven sons, bury an infant daughter and raise three orphaned boys on their farm in the North Central Texas community of Plano. Lizzie's mother, sisters and brothers joined the Carpenters and an older brother in Texas in 1857. Lizzie not only wrote about her own family's activities over the years, but also activities of other family members and an increasing number of friends to create a lasting record of a pioneer woman's life.

When preparing the quilts and journal entries for *Gone to Texas,* my first book based on Lizzie Carpenter's seven journals, it became increasingly apparent that so much information was left untouched. Reading and rereading the entries Lizzie wrote over a 25 year period from 1857-1882, images jumped off the page revealing snapshots of daily life. The relevance of the seasons, cycles of life and the repetition of tasks – all simple matters of fact for daily life of a pioneer family – were recorded almost daily in Lizzie's journals, which she called her record of work. So many tasks were taken for granted and simply completed without note. While her words were not all about work, the description of such is prominent. Work as recorded centered around the Carpenter homestead. The comings and goings of friends and hired help, various crops, the prairie where cattle roamed and the sheep, horses and later donkeys that stayed closer to home, as did hogs, geese, chickens and Old Speck, the dairy cow, all played a role in Lizzie's record.

The Carpenter farm was a fairly independent entity, relying on crops and stock to provide nourishment and clothing for the family as well as income. Lizzie's work in the home making the family's clothes and bedding, making clothes for others, tending the vegetable garden, hiving bees and selling butter all served as her contribution to the family's income and well being.

Lizzie's home near Plano, Texas. Robert is the second man from the right, and next to him is second wife Nellie. The house was built around the original cabin, shown in the back.

For Everything there is a Season

Just as the planting, tending and harvesting of crops had their seasons, so did Lizzie's sewing, weaving, knitting and quilting. Every task had its time, whether repeated daily, weekly, monthly, seasonally or yearly and were interdependent upon previous tasks.

To make clothes, for example, months of preparation would precede it. When Lizzie was ready to cut out and sew wool pants for the boys or Mr. Carpenter, months prior the sheep had to be sheared in the Spring, then it would take weeks to pick the wool clean of debris. Once cleaned, the wool needed to be carded by hand or by machine. After carding was completed, the wool would then be spun into yarn, some for knitting, and the rest for the loom. Before the wool could be woven, days and weeks would be spent at the spinning wheel – spinning and twisting the wool for thread or yarn – and then wool was dyed the desired color. Once the wool was spun and dyed, and the warp loaded on the loom, days would be spent weaving, the resulting wool cloth would then be ready, months later, to be cut out for pants.

Quilts would be quilted when Lizzie had cotton for batting. To get to that point, cotton had to be planted and picked months before, both dependent on favorable weather. After picking cotton in the fields, it had to be carded and then patted into a batting and the rest spun and twisted into thread for a variety of purposes, including the warp in the loom to weave with wool for "lincy" – the warp and weft woven into cloth for sheets or clothing or thread to be dyed for the jeans or cloth for sheets or for sewing and quilting thread. The better the crop, the more cotton could be saved for future battings.

Lizzie Carpenter

Lizzie and Robert Carpenter

Kate and Clint Haggard, Lizzie's sister and her husband, frequent guests in the Carpenter home. Clint was one of Robert's best friends.

How this Book is Organized

The quilts for *Lizzie's Legacy* are inspired by Lizzie's writing and are presented within chapters that illustrate various aspects of pioneer life – friendship, chores, the help and guests, insects and pastimes. Within each chapter, the journal entries are organized chronologically. Occasionally, there are entries that apply to more than one chapter. These entries offer insight into day-to-day life, the sameness of the seasons, the strict routine necessary to keep the farm running and the endless cycle of work to keep the family fed, clothed, warmed and sheltered. Guests and hired help were welcomed, fed and sheltered as well. While all aspects intertwine to define work, "knocking around," probably called "piddling around" today, was also noted along with visits to family and friends, giving a respite from the routine.

Going to Sunday School and church meetings offered opportunities to gather or "pic nic" and share a meal with friends or family. A simple ride out on the prairie, "to try out my new saddle," was a welcome break from a long day's work. Playing baseball or hunting or fishing offered a respite for the men and boys, while organizing social parties for sewing, quilting or a game of croquet offered the women some entertainment.

The wrath of Mother Nature was a constant worry when too much or not enough rain, or grasshoppers, or a hail storm could determine success or failure of a crop, and hence Lizzie's productivity and the welfare of the family in general.

As you read the entries, remember Lizzie was writing to her dear friend, her journal, sharing her days' thoughts often in random fragments that had little or no punctuation. Spellings changed from month to month, even the names of her sons.

A Legacy to be Remembered

Thankfully, Lizzie's journals are archived in the Plano Library. Regrettably, none of her quilts or other textiles exist. It has been a pleasure, a labor of love, to recreate Lizzie's quilts as inspired by her writings. Lizzie's quiltmaking was extensive, yet few quilts were given names and even fewer described. Quilts were, however, divided into categories: cradle quilts, quilts for the little bed, quilts for the lounge, comforts, and quilts, which I assume were for the larger beds. All the quilts would then be divided by fabric type, worsted (wool), lincy (linsey-woolsey), yarn (flannel), silk and calico. To recreate her quilts and those she helped quilt, it was similar to solving a mystery, gathering clues here and there to determine what the quilt might have looked like and then make it in fabrics suitable for the time period with today's reproduction fabrics. Lizzie's quilts were made to be used, even though some were "quilted close." Lizzie made quilts out of necessity to keep her family warm, but truly enjoyed each one she made. In a very characteristic statement made September 9, 1871, Lizzie wrote, "I have all my sewing done that is needful just now. I reckon I can work on some quilts." Lizzie did just that – *lots* of quilts.

Carpenter sons
In birth order **seated left to right: William Joel, Gipson Edgar, John Henry, Jefferson Davis**
Standing left to right: Robert Elzie, Benjamin Owen, Edward Albert and Gano (Robert's son with 2nd wife Nellie)

CHAPTER 1

Kindred Friendship

Lizzie spent so much of her time with men and boys that every moment spent with her mother, sisters, sisters-in-law or friends was quite treasured. Besides her husband Robert, her seven sons and the three orphaned boys she raised, a number of men often came to the farm. Some came frequently to purchase stock while others arrived to assist in the harvesting of various crops. Travelers, peddlers, boarders and hired help came and went constantly. They stayed overnight and had to be fed. Lizzie wrote "hope they make themselves scarce before I go about dinner."

Whether the ladies shared time quilting or visiting, the ties between these women were strong and important for Lizzie's well being. She longed for female companionship and would not miss a quilting opportunity if at all possible. These gatherings offered a time to talk and share thoughts, and maybe get a get some quilting done, too.

1857

June 2 Helped Mary Ann quilt on a comfort.

1858

March 19 Mr Yeager and wife and my humble self went to Ma's to help on Kate's quilt – made Mr Carpenter a shirt in the morning

August 25 Sewed a little – done some baking for my sewing party – cut out several garments

26 Had a little sociable sewing party of Mrs and Miss Lunsford, Mrs Mathews and Mrs Givens

1860

May 31 Went to Ben's to help Mary Ann quilt she has Mrs Sheppard's quilt in Ma went to help

1861

March 12 Went to Ma's to help Sister on her block quilt

1872

April 29 Mr C, myself and some of the boys went to Kate Haggard's to a quilting – good many persons there

1874

April 2 This is a beautiful day Mother and myself went to see Sister Mary Brown. We found them well and prosperous. I worked on Vina Taylors quilt – peaced basket – I am setting it together for her.

3 This morning I made some garden – planted beets and radishes. This is a very pretty day. Mrs Lou Judge came to see me this evening – I was glad to see her – she is pleasant company – Worked on Vina's quilt to day

4 This has been a very windy day, one that March borrowed and paid back to April. John and I picked the geese this morning. I looked for Kate Haggard this evening but she did not come – I wish she had, it has been so long since she was here.

April 6 worked on Vina's quilt in the evening

7 Sewed on Vina's basket quilt in the morning

8 Finished Vina's quilt (top)

10 took Vina's quilt home

21 went up to Mr Judges – helped Mrs Judge quilt

May 4 this morning I made several pillowcases and a bolster tick and filled them this evening I put in a quilt for Vina – basket pattern

6 Ma came down this morning to help me quilt – Aronia Crozier and Adelia Brown and Mary Ann also came over I was glad to see them also glad to have their help which they gladly gave.

15 I must set a hen then go to quilting – have been quilting steady to day – quilted a large border – been rather lonesome. Mr C and Mr Leer started to Dallas with some horses

22 To day I finished my carpet, put it down and fixed things up in the new room and put in another quilt – I am expecting here Lady friends tomorrow to help me quilt – Two men here to-night to stay overnight with us – lightening rod men

23 This has been a pleasant day – quite a few Ladies here – we had a very pleasant day – finished Vina's quilt and quilted two or three rolls on my plated hexicon hexigon

1880

January 13 I went to Mary Ann's to a quilting party – there were a good many ladies there – had a nice time and good dinner. Effie Mathews and Minnie Harrington here – I was glad to have the young ladies company

Sisters Block Quilt

MADE AND QUILTED BY BETSY CHUTCHIAN

36 ³/₄" x 42 ¹/₂"

5 ¹/₄" x 6" FINISHED BLOCK

Lizzie helped her sister, Mary Susanna, with this quilt in March of 1861. At this same time, Lizzie was expecting my great grandfather and was working on a hexagon quilt, featured in *Gone to Texas*. Both quilts use the same technique – English Paper Piecing. Today, I enjoy this technique for its portable nature.

Fabrics

1 ½ yards total assorted light prints
1 ½ yards total assorted medium prints
1 ½ yards total assorted dark prints
1 ⅔ yard for backing
¼ yard for binding

Cutting

Note: The templates are provided on page 17. When making the templates, add a generous ¼" seam allowance to each. If you prefer to use pre-made templates, use the 3" Six-Pointed Diamond by Paper Pieces (found at www.paperpieces.com).

From the assorted light prints, cut:
59 of Template 1
8 of Template 2
6 of Template 3
1 of Template 4
1 of Template 5

From assorted medium prints, cut:
63 of Template 1

From assorted dark prints, cut:
63 of Template 1
6 of Template 3
1 of Template 4
1 of Template 5

Block Assembly

1. Prepare paper shapes for English Paper Piecing by basting fabric over each paper shape.

   Place paper template on wrong side of fabric, secure with a pin allowing a ¼" seam allowance all around. Trim using sharp scissors. Fold one seam over the template and secure with small paper clip. Remove the pin.

   Begin basting on either side of the paper clip. Fold under the corners as you stitch. Baste through the fabric and paper. Remove the paper clip as you approach the last corner. Backstitch to end.

   Follow same procedure for the other shapes.

    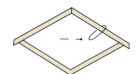

2. Whip stitch together 1 light diamond, 1 medium diamond, and 1 dark diamond as shown.

   Make 59 blocks

3. Whip stitch together 1 light triangle and 1 medium diamond as shown.

   Make 4

4. Whip stitch together 1 light triangle and 1 dark diamond as shown.

   Make 4

Quilt Top Assembly

1. Arrange the blocks and partial blocks as shown in quilt diagram.

2. Join blocks with a whip stitch in rows, and then join rows. Remove the papers as you go after the shape has been surrounded by other shapes.

Finishing

Sister's Block Quilt is tied with perle cotton in an X at each corner intersection. Bind with 1 ⅛" single fold binding.

Templates

*Add a generous ¼" seam allowance to each template.

Template 1

Assembly Diagram

Template 2

Template 3

Template 4

Template 5

Friendship Baskets

MADE BY BETSY CHUTCHIAN AND FRIENDS
QUILTED BY SHERI MECOM
65" x 78 ½"
32 BLOCKS – 7" FINISHED

For this quilt, I was inspired by Lizzie's journal entries for the quiltings she hosted and those she attended. I asked members of my stitch group, Patchwork Piecers, if they would like to, not just make some blocks for the quilt, but to have a block exchange so that by the time the book was published they would have their blocks ready to set. Gathering together to visit while we stitch is the best part of my group – laughter is rampant, sometimes there are tears, some sewing is occasionally accomplished, but oh what fun we have!

These moments are what Lizzie longed to have when surrounded so often by nothing but men and boys. Seven friends made two blocks each for my quilt and I made blocks for them as well, then I made more to reach the quilt size I desired. Lizzie helped her friend, Vina Taylor, with her basket quilt in the spring of 1874. The antique basket blocks (shown on page 20) are not Lizzie's unfortunately, nor Vina's. In 2009, I found the blocks in an antique shop in Galveston, Texas shortly after Hurricane Ike hit the Texas coast in 2008.

Fabrics

2 yards light cream solid
1 ¼ yards total assorted madder red, orange, and brown prints
1 ½ yards rust for sashing
1 ⅝ yards blue for cornerstones, setting triangles, corner triangles, border corners and binding
1 ⅜ yards for border, 2 yards if cutting lengthwise
4 ¾ yards for backing

Cutting

From cream solid, cut:
32 – 1 ½" squares (A)
208 – 1 ⅞" squares, cut each once on the diagonal (B)
16 – 3 ¼" squares, cut each twice on the diagonal (C)
32 – 3 ⅞" squares, cut each once on the diagonal (D)
64 – 2 ½" x 4 ½" rectangles (E)

From assorted madder red, orange and browns, cut:
320 – 1 ⅞" squares, cut each once on the diagonal (G)
16 – 3 ⅞" squares, cut each once on the diagonal (H)

From rust sashing, cut:
80 – 3" x 7 ½" rectangles

From blue setting print, cut:
31 – 3" cornerstones
5 – 4 ⅞" squares, cut each twice on the diagonal for half cornerstones
4 – 11 ⅛" squares, cut each twice on the diagonal for side triangles
2 – 6" squares, cut each once on the diagonal (this is slightly oversized for trimming)
8 – 2 ¼" x the width of fabric for double fold binding
4 – 5 ½" squares for outer corners

From border print, cut:
4 – 5 ½" strips cut lengthwise or 8 strips the width of fabric

Block Assembly

1. Make 13 half square triangle units by sewing 13 cream triangles (B) to 13 dark triangles (G) Press to the dark.

2. Sew 1 cream triangle (C) to 1 dark triangle (G) as shown below. Press to the cream.

Sew 1 cream triangle (C) to the opposite side of 1 dark triangle (G) in a mirror image of the first set. Press to the dark.

3. Assemble the basket handle unit as shown in the diagrams. The arrows show pressing directions.

⟵ Press

⟶ Press

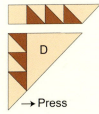 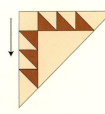

⟶ Press

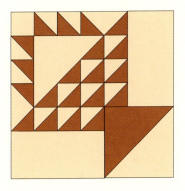 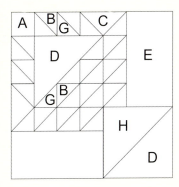

4. Assemble the left side of basket base by placing 6 triangle units and 4 dark triangles (G) in rows and sew together as shown in the diagrams.

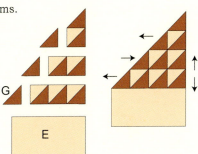

5. Assemble the right side of basket base by sewing one row of 3 triangle units to 1 triangle (G). Then, sew that row to rectangle (E) as shown in diagrams below. Press to the rectangle (E). Sew 1 H triangle and 1 D triangle together.

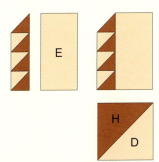

6. Sew the H/D half square triangle unit to the bottom of the Step 5 unit. Press to the H/D unit. Sew left side unit and right side unit together.

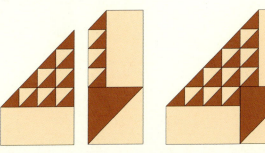

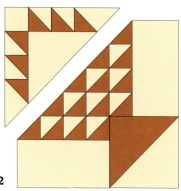

7. Join handle and base sections.

Make 32

Quilt Assembly

1. Referring to quilt diagram join sashing to half cornerstones and cornerstone squares, in diagonal rows. Press to cornerstones. Also, join sashing strips to blocks and side triangles. Press to cornerstones.

2. Join diagonal rows together, pressing to sashing rows.

3. Add 4 corner triangles to top. Trim edges and corners if needed, allowing ¼" seam on all sides.

4. Measure the quilt top from top to bottom through middle of quilt. Piece border strips to match that measurement for sides of quilt. Stitch, then press to border.

5. Measure quilt top, side to side through the middle. Piece border strips to match that measurement. Join corner squares to each end of those strips. Stitch top and bottom borders to quilt top.

Finishing

Friendship Baskets is beautifully custom quilted with cables in the border, feathers in the setting triangles, pumpkin seeds in the cornerstones and a double rod pattern for the blocks and sashing. It is bound with double fold binding.

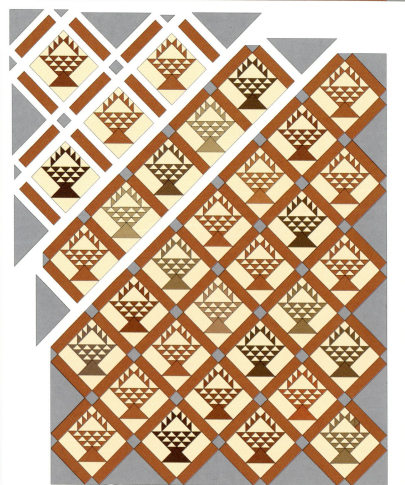

Assembly Diagram

CHAPTER 2

Doing Chores

By definition, chores are routine tasks or jobs, sometimes difficult or disagreeable, but necessary. Early Texas pioneers, in their efforts to be self-sufficient, found that not just the everyday chores recurred, but there were weekly, monthly and yearly tasks that had to be done to keep the household and farm running. Every task was scheduled. Crops were planted seasonally according to the Farmers' Almanac. Milking cows and feeding horses and other stock was daily. Hogs were killed when very cold in November and December. Churning, cooking, doing dishes and sweeping were also daily tasks. Every member of the family had responsibilities.

Bedding was scalded monthly, often twice a month and linens and clothes were washed weekly and sometimes more often, until Lizzie found in 1879 that she could wash every two weeks. Schedules were established for cutting out and sewing all garments for every member of the Carpenter household, family, slaves and hired help. Shearing sheep occurred every spring so picking, carding and spinning of the wool soon followed so knitting and weaving could be done. Geese were picked periodically for bed and pillow ticks. Crops of wheat, oats, corn and cotton had ever rotating cycles of plowing, planting and harvesting, dependent completely on weather conditions.

As Lizzie kept her record of work, these chores were noted. In her account totaling the year's work, she would often write "patching and gardening and other tasks too numerous to mention, is omitted." Lizzie valued her work as contributing to the welfare of her family and apologized when she could not live up to a standard set for herself.

Jefferson D. Carpenter

John H. Carpenter

1857

July 28 Got dinner and cleaned up. Churned etc washed some in the evening

October 21 cut carpet rags and carded some in the evening

23 carded and spun some and twisted some in the evening

December 9 made some sheets and a pair of pillow slips cut out some shirts

1858

June 10 Got dinner – Milla and Jane at Spring Creek washing

14 washed a big washing Mary helped me set my blue dye

June 26 spun some for my jeans

Butter profits for June 1858
June 5 – 5 1/2 lbs to Plano 55 cents
June 12 – 9 lbs to Plano 90 cents
June 19 – 10 lbs to Plano 1.00
June 26 – 10 lbs to Plano 1.00
Purchased glasses and dishes 1.05

1862

May 8 picked wool and got very tired of it – think I will quit picking the white

19 Feel pretty feeble but do a big weeks work to make up for last week

27 Carded and spun sewing thread

1863

January 17 Willie and I had to watch the sheep – 2 pigs got out of the run and killed 2 lambs

March (date unreadable) I went out this morning and drove up Old Speck – found her – Buffalo Creek

1866

April 28 the past week I have been busied in various ways – carded and spun a little, sewed some and picked some wool – I also went to Ma's to help her quilt – Mr Carpenter sheared his sheep last week and now I am very busy or will be until I get my wool ready for the (card) machine.

June 12 This the first harvesting (wheat) in our neighborhood – my garden looks well and I will have an abundance of vegetables soon – to day is wash day and I must quit writing – for tis my fate to be cook on wash day

October 6 I have my lincy filling spun and colored and in the coming week I wish to spin for my jeans

1867

October 20 I must try to spin some the coming week for winter will soon be here and little boys need their winter clothing – Made my green tomato catsup

1869

April 18 My old cook has gone and I have the cooking to do in addition to my other work, what with the babe to tend is no light job

May 6 this week with the help of my sewing machine I made Willy and Gippy, Johny and Jeffy a pair of pants apiece and Tobe a pair and finished Rene a dress. Done a big washing and Ironing and cooking for the family

June 12 The past week I made Gippie a pair of pants and a coat and Easter Gambol a bonnet – a cover for the buggy and run up a bed tick for the lounge – washed bed clothes and covers

October 17 Monday I finished picking wool – I have not done as much as usual and kept busy too – I have spun 16 cuts of yarn doubled and twisted some of it and made myself and Bennie a sack

November 2 I have been cooking, washing, Ironing, sewing and spinning – I am nearly done spinning

1871

March 12 Men and boys company for dinner – After I got the dinner dishes put away, I took a walk up in the orchard to look at its beauties, the trees are in full bloom and it is not often we see a prettier sight than is there displayed – some of the trees are covered with deep pink, some pale, and some are almost white with beautiful blooms while here and there we see one that has shed its bloom and are covered with the most beautiful little green leaves. I have never seen a more flattering prospect of fruit.

June 18 made 15 garments in 2 weeks spooled and warped piece of carpet Mr Patton came to board

continued on page 31

Picking Geese

PIECED AND HAND QUILTED BY BETSY CHUTCHIAN

63 ³/₄" X 76 ¹/₂"

28 – 9" FINISHED BLOCKS

4 HALF BLOCKS

The antique version of this quilt, shown on page 30, is owned by a dear friend, Pat Prestridge of San Antonio, Texas. I first fell in love with this quilt before writing *Gone to Texas*. Pat displays this quilt in her breakfast room each Fall along with lovely collections of dishes and artwork. Treasured friend, fabulous 1870's quilt – I couldn't wait to replicate it as closely as possible.

The block is known by several names: *Devil's Claw* is one, as is *Brown Goose,* as Pat calls it. Being a brown goose goes well with Lizzie's journal entries about picking geese for feathers and down to fill the many pillows and bed ticks (mattresses) needed regularly for all the beds.

Fabrics
For Blocks

2 yards total assorted brown and red prints
2 yards total assorted light prints

For Zigzag Setting

1 ½ yard stripe (if desired)
1 ⅝ yard assorted stripes in madder reds, madder browns, and soft browns (3 ⅛ yards total if not using a stripe fabric)
5 yards backing
⅝ yard binding

Cutting
For Blocks

The cutting instructions are for 2 blocks. You will need 28 blocks and 4 half blocks.

From the light prints, cut:

3 squares 5 ¾" – cut each twice on the diagonal (A)
4 squares 3 ⅛" – cut each once on the diagonal (B)

From the dark prints, cut:

3 squares 5 ¾" – cut each twice on the diagonal (C)
4 squares 3 ⅛" – cut each twice on the diagonal (D)

For Zigzag Setting

The stripe is cut for effect, like the antique quilt, leaving bias edges on the outside of the quilt. Take care when cutting and follow the photo closely. If not using a stripe, follow the cutting directions below.

From the stripe, cut:

Cut 9 squares 9 ⅞" – cut each once on the diagonal for the setting triangles

Cut 3 squares 10 ¼" – cut each twice on the diagonal for the corners

From madder reds and browns, cut:

9 squares 14" – cut each twice on the diagonal

If not using a stripe fabric, cut:

14 – 14" squares, cut each twice on the diagonal to make 54 setting triangles. (Two will not be used.)

6 squares 7 ¼" – cut each once on the diagonal to make 12 corner triangles.

Block assembly

Full Block

1. Following the diagram below, join 2 triangles (A) and 2 triangles (C) together for center.

2. Then sew 4 triangles (D) to 2 triangles (A) and sew to top and bottom of center unit.

3. Join 4 triangles (C) to 2 triangles (A) and sew to sides of unit assembled above. Lastly, add the 4 corner triangles (B) to unit.

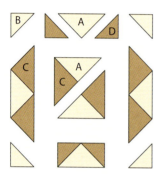

Make 18

Half block

1. Following the diagram below, assemble triangles in units. Join 1 triangle (B) to 1 triangle (C).

2. Sew 2 triangles (D) to either side of 1 triangle (A). Sew 1 triangle (A) to 1 triangle (C). Sew the two units together.

3. Sew 2 triangles (C) to 1 triangle (A) side unit. Lastly, add 2 triangles (B) to unit.

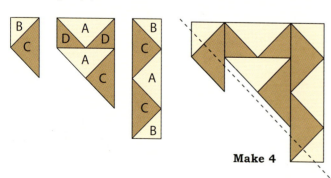

Make 4

Trim excess keeping ¼" seam allowance, stay stitch the bias edge, just inside seam allowance

Vertical row assembly

1. Assemble strips of blocks in diagonal rows as shown below. If working with a stripe to follow the quilt photo for placement of the stripes.

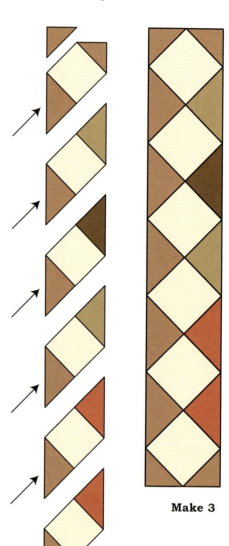

Make 3

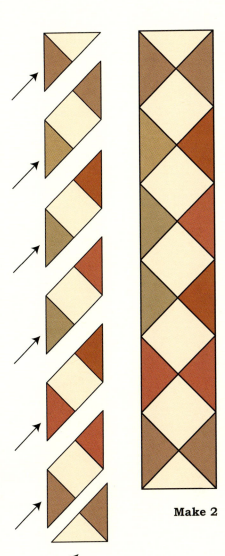

Sew rows together matching midpoint of setting triangle to corner of block.

Once the rows are joined, trim across top and bottom, keeping ¼" seam. Stay stitch the edges carefully by hand to prevent stretching before quilting.

Make 2

Finishing

Picking Geese is hand quilted with size 8 perle cotton in utility quilting style, in parallel lines following the zigzag pattern of the setting and simple outlines defining the chevron shapes within the block.

Utility quilting designs are usually simple with larger stitches than fine hand quilting. Quilts such as this one would have been made to be used daily. Utility style quilting gives the pleasure of fine hand quilting in far less time. Bind in 2 ¼" double fold binding.

Assembly Diagram

continued from page 25

1872

May 26 Watching for Willie and Eddie to take the measles – Pick the geese, cook and sweep, company here all week

June 3 Willes right sick with the measles – Eddie has them but don't seem to be very sick though he is broke out pretty thick – cooked for the harvest hands

September 12 Made willy 2 shirts helped Mother quilt on day picked my geese and made two satchels for the boys to take to school

September 23 Mr Carpenter has been very busy for sometime gathering corn, he has no one to help him but John and Jeffy and they have to churn and help me of a morning before they can go out – he has about finished one piece and then he is a goodeal more than half done – his corn is very good this year

October 21 Johny and Jeffy are picking cotton

November 26 Mrs Bush and Mrs Fulgham came over to me a little while – they caught me pretty dirty for we killed hogs yesterday and I had been busied cooking up my lard and fixing sausage – but I was glad to see them and soon cleaned myself up a little.

1874

June 27 I and John picked geese this morning – I must make Eddie a dress this evening and clean up the house.

July 29 To day Martha washed I got dinner. The menfolk were hunting up cattle to sell for beef – some half a dozen of the men came in for dinner at about half past two o'clock so I did not do much settled work today

September 3 Johny and myself picked geese this morning.

October 3 Saturday – Day of all work. Clean, mend bake etc Martha has gone to Dallas and I am cook and waiting maid generally until she comes back – four men here besides our own family to do for which makes it pretty heavy.

November 13 I finished Gippies pants and commenced a pair for John sewing mostly on my hands and get along pretty slow – pants sewn on the machine will rip (a Wheeler and Wilson, her second sewing machine)

November 16 I cut out 10 garments this morning – pants and drawers – sewed some on pants for Jeffy

December 2 I have been busy at various jobs today – twisted some thread for yarn and am going to color it this evening.

1876

February 7 This morning I quilted some – in the evening I and Martha picked geese – Martha White came down this evening and I sewed a little for her on the machine – she in turn helped us pick geese.

1878

May 6 As I have no help this week I thought I would have the washing done up early in the week so I got Jeff to wash on the machine and I bossed and helped some – I got dinner and cleaned up everything and have made me some dewberry preserves

June 23 Ma and several gentlemen came home with us to dinner – It is getting late and I will quilt now and help Bobbie to milk

November 6 I am very busy these days and I call it busy doing nothing for I do not get any settled work done except a little knitting or mending – as I am doing the cooking and all the kitchen work and washing also with the boys help – they work the washer and wringer while I do the rest with the Ironing – so I find very little time for sewing

November 14 Yesterday Mr C and I picked the geese.

December 8 I want to get my sewing done before Christmas so I can piece some quilts

continued on page 36

Selling Butter

PIECED AND HAND QUILTED BY BETSY CHUTCHIAN

18" x 18"

4" FINISHED BLOCK

Lizzie recorded her work in daily journal entries proving the contribution she made to the household income. It is odd that churning butter is rarely mentioned, but the records of pounds of butter sold to stores in town are frequent. Besides selling butter, Lizzie also sold wool from the sheep she and Mr. Carpenter raised, and she was also paid to make garments for men and women.

Fabrics

For Blocks

⅛ yard each of 4 indigo prints
¼ yard light print or shirting

For setting and backing

¼ yard indigo for sash and binding
Fat quarter indigo for setting triangles
⅔ yard backing

Cutting

From the light print, cut:
2 – 2 ½" squares (A)
1 – 1 ½" square (B)
4 – 1 ¼" x 1 ½" rectangles (C)
1 – 1 ¼" square for the cornerstone

From indigo prints, cut:
2 – 2 ½" squares (D)
4 – 1 ¼" x 1 ½" rectangles (E)
4 – 1 ¼" x 4 ½" for the sashing
2 – 7 ⅛" squares. Cut each once on the diagonal for the setting corners.

Block assembly

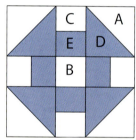

1. Pair 2 indigo squares (D) with 2 light squares (A). Draw diagonal line and sew ¼" on each side of line. Cut apart on drawn line. Press to the dark. Trim to 2" x 2".

Make 4

2. Sew 4 indigo rectangles (E) to light rectangles (C). Press seams open.

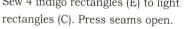

Make 4

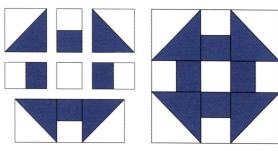

Make 4 blocks

3. Arrange in rows and sew together. Join the rows. Press to one side.

Quilt top assembly

1. Join blocks to sashing as shown.

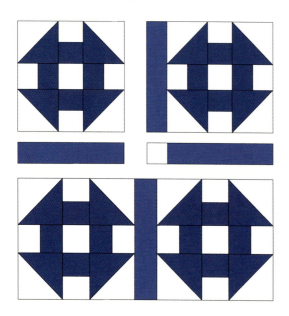

2. Add 4 indigo triangles to the 4 corners.

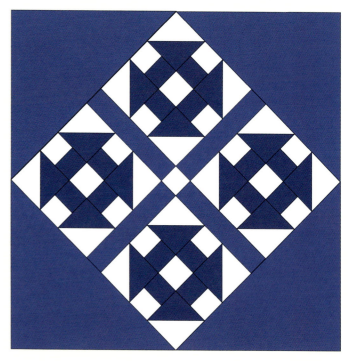

Assembly Diagram

Finishing

Selling Butter is hand quilted and bound in a narrow 1 ⅛" single fold binding.

continued from page 31

1879

May 28 Just finished up the washing with John's help. Did not wash last week and think I will adopt that plan ... It will only take up one half day of the boys time from the field

June 30 Emma has come down with Willie now that the thresher has moved here to our wheat – guess I will have them a while to cook for – well I hope I may keep able to do it – I must go and gather up the clothes and make the beds up stairs and fix them for the thresher hands and then get supper.

1880

February 24 Jeff and I washed this morning – and dinner is over and things cleaned up – I want to plant a little corn for early roasting ears

August 11 Wednesday Lou and I finished the quilt Monday that I had in for some time – We have been threshing here since Monday – I am pretty tired as I had to get dinner for all without any help except for the little boys

December 31 In the year that closes, I have made about 86 garments, quilted 3 quilts, 1 comfort and pieced 3 or finished up that many that had been commenced before. I also done the principal part of Ironing – cooking – and housework as I have had no hired help this year.

1881

February 8 Bobbie and I have just finished picking the geese always a dreaded job though its not much work after one gets at it.

March 13 We are getting a heap of milk now and make a goodeal of butter – I have sent 34 lbs to town this year.

May 31 Hail storm ruined the cotton crop

Twist & Spin

MADE BY BETSY CHUTCHIAN
QUILTED BY SHERI MECOM
33 ³/₄" x 42 ¹/₂"
12 – 6 ¹/₄" FINISHED BLOCKS

Endless hours were spent spinning both wool and cotton. The shearing of sheep, picking cotton, picking the wool clean and the carding of both wool and cotton preceeded the many hours spent at the spinning wheel. Lizzie wrote so often, year after year, of these very necessary chores. Spun cotton thread would be used for sewing or the warp in the loom for rugs, blankets or sheets. Spun wool could be doubled and twisted for knitting socks and stockings or for the weaving the fabric Lizzie called worsted – or to make blankets. The quilt block pattern is called *Single Wedding Ring* or *Crown of Thorns*, but to me the blocks resemble the spinning of the wheel.

Fabrics

2 yards total assorted (8 or more) pink prints
2 ¼ yards cream print for blocks and setting and pieced border
¼ yard pink print for 1 ⅛" single fold binding

Cutting

From the pinks, cut:
48 – 1 ¾" squares (B)
206 – 2 ¼" squares for half square triangle units (D)
4 – 1 ⅛" x width of fabric strips for single fold binding

From the cream print, cut:
60 – 1 ¾" squares (A)
206 – 2 ¼" squares for half square triangle units (C)
6 – 6 ¾" squares for alternate squares
3 – 10 ¼" squares – cut each twice on the diagonal for the side triangles
2 – 5 ½" squares – cut each once on the diagonal for the corners
4 – 1 ¾" x the width of fabric strips for border

Block assembly

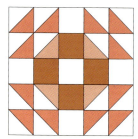 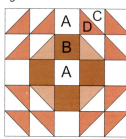

1. Make 16 half-square triangle units from 8 cream squares (C) and 8 pink squares (D)

Sew ¼" on each side of drawn diagonal line. Cut apart on drawn line. Press to the pink. Trim to 1 ¾".

2. Following the diagram below, sew the triangle units to 5 cream squares (A) and 4 pink squares (B) in rows. Follow pressing arrows for each row. Then join the 5 rows together as shown.

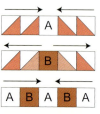

Make 12 blocks

Quilt top assembly

1. Referring to quilt assembly diagram on page 41, join blocks with setting squares and triangles in diagonal rows.

2. Join rows together.

3. Trim edges keeping a ¼" seam allowance.

Borders

1. Using the directions from Block Assembly Step 1, page 38, make 164 half-square triangle units from the cream (C) and the pink squares (D). Trim units to 1 ¾".

2. For the sides of the pieced inner border, sew 2 strips of 28 units as shown in the quilt assembly diagram on page 41. Sew to the sides of top.

3. For the top and bottom borders sew 2 strips of 23 triangle units. Sew to the top and bottom.

4. For the middle border, sew the 1 ¾" x 35 ½" cream side strips to each side of quilt top. Sew the 1 ¾" x 29 ¼" cream top and bottom strips to top and bottom of quilt top. Press to the cream strips.

5. For the outer pieced border, sew 2 strips of 32 triangle units for sides. For the top and bottom, sew 2 strips of 27 triangle units.

6. Sew the pieced strips, first to sides, then to top and bottom. Press to the cream border.

Finishing

Twist and Spin is custom quilted with feathered wreaths in the blocks and a floral design in the setting and bound with single fold binding in pink.

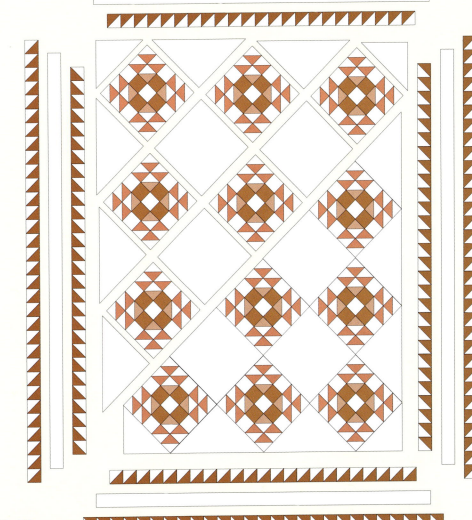

Assembly Diagram

So Many Dishes

Lizzie was quite fortunate to have help with the household chores for most of her married life. Having help permitted her to have time for sewing, quilting and visits to friends and family. However, on washing day, Lizzie was, as she put it, "chief cook" and at harvest time, when men would come to the farm with the thresher, or to pick cotton, and there would be so many hands for dinner that she had to help prepare meals. So many mouths to feed left so many dishes to wash. By the time meals were prepared and the dishes cleaned, Lizzie would complain that it left her little time for "settled work." Lizzie would always rather be sewing or quilting! After the loss of her babe, Mary Katie, in 1878, Lizzie had very little help and found she did very well by herself. The block pattern for *So Many Dishes* is a Broken Dishes variation.

Fabrics

⅝ yard total assorted light prints or shirtings
⅝ yard total assorted indigo prints for blocks
¾ yard of one indigo print for setting and binding
⅝ yard of a second indigo for border
1 ⅜ yard backing

Cutting

From assorted indigo prints, cut:
20 – 2" squares (A)
40 – 2 ½" squares – cut each once on the diagonal (B)
120 – 1 ¾" squares – cut each once on the diagonal (C)

From assorted light prints, cut:
40 – 2" squares – cut each once on the diagonal (D)
80 – 1 ¼" x 2" rectangles (E)
120 – 1 ¾" squares – cut each once on the diagonal (F)

From setting fabric, cut:
12 – 5" squares
4 – 7 ¾" squares – cut each twice on the diagonal
2 – 4 ¼" square – cut each once on the diagonal
4 – 1 ⅛" x the width of fabric strips for single fold binding

From border fabric, cut:
4 – 4 ½" x the width of fabric strips

Block assembly

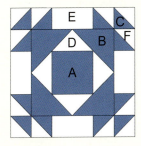

1. Sew triangles (D) to sides of center (A). Press to the light.

2. Add the triangles (B) to the corners. Press to the indigo. Trim to 3 ½".

3. Sew light and indigo triangles (C) and (F) together to make 12 half square triangle units. Press the seams open. Trim to 1 ¼".

4. Sew 1 half-square triangle unit to each end of rectangle (E). Press to the light.

Make 2

5. Sew these units to sides as shown.

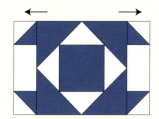

6. Sew 2 half-square triangle units to each end of rectangle (E).

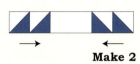

Make 2

7. Sew these units to the top and bottom as shown.

Make 20 blocks

Borders

Trim the quilt top edges even maintaining ¼" seam allowance. Measure the quilt top lengthwise through the middle and cut 2 – 4 ½" indigo strips to match that measurement. Sew these strips to each side of top. Press to border.

Next measure quit top crosswise through the middle and cut 2 - 4 ½" indigo strips to match that measurement. Sew these strips to top and bottom of top. Press to border.

Quilt top assembly

Arrange 20 blocks in a pleasing manner with 12 setting squares, 14 setting triangles and 4 corner triangles as shown in the quilt assembly diagram. Sew in diagonal rows. Join rows together. Trim edges together, keeping a ¼" seam allowance.

Finishing

So Many Dishes is quilted in an allover paisley design with a single fold indigo binding.

Assembly Diagram

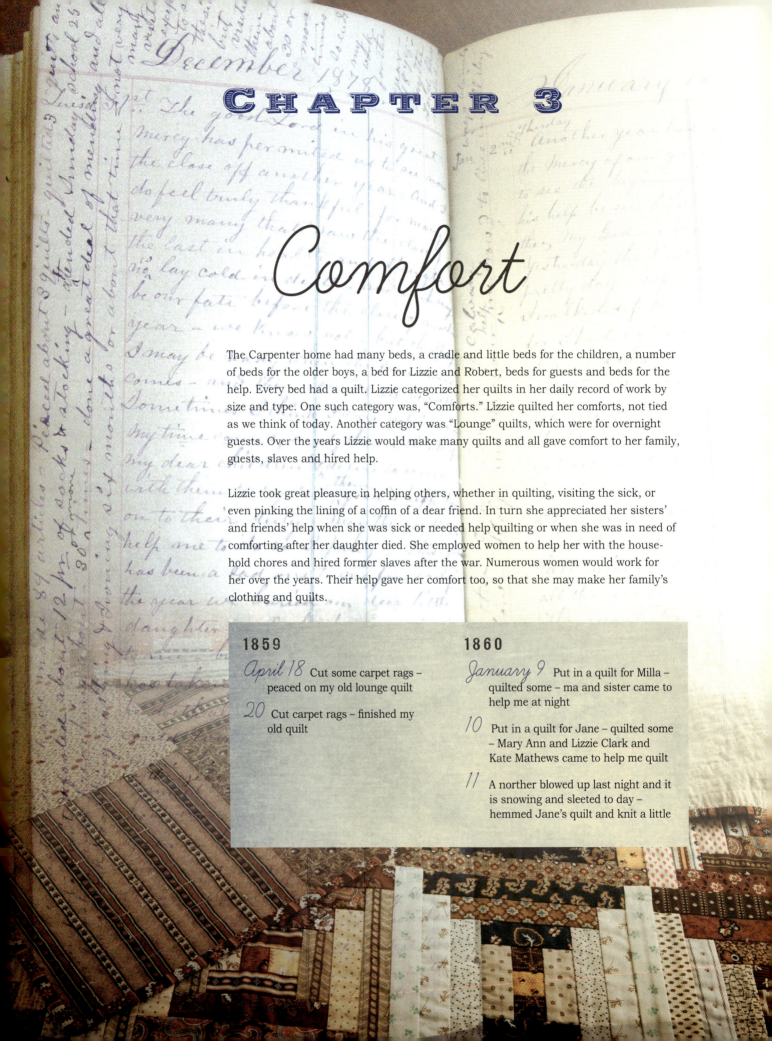

CHAPTER 3

Comfort

The Carpenter home had many beds, a cradle and little beds for the children, a number of beds for the older boys, a bed for Lizzie and Robert, beds for guests and beds for the help. Every bed had a quilt. Lizzie categorized her quilts in her daily record of work by size and type. One such category was, "Comforts." Lizzie quilted her comforts, not tied as we think of today. Another category was "Lounge" quilts, which were for overnight guests. Over the years Lizzie would make many quilts and all gave comfort to her family, guests, slaves and hired help.

Lizzie took great pleasure in helping others, whether in quilting, visiting the sick, or even pinking the lining of a coffin of a dear friend. In turn she appreciated her sisters' and friends' help when she was sick or needed help quilting or when she was in need of comforting after her daughter died. She employed women to help her with the household chores and hired former slaves after the war. Numerous women would work for her over the years. Their help gave her comfort too, so that she may make her family's clothing and quilts.

1859

April 18 Cut some carpet rags – peaced on my old lounge quilt

20 Cut carpet rags – finished my old quilt

1860

January 9 Put in a quilt for Milla – quilted some – ma and sister came to help me at night

10 Put in a quilt for Jane – quilted some – Mary Ann and Lizzie Clark and Kate Mathews came to help me quilt

11 A norther blowed up last night and it is snowing and sleeted to day – hemmed Jane's quilt and knit a little

1861

January 28 Peaced on my worsted cradle quilt – put in and quilted Milla a quilt – Ma and Sister helped me

February 18 worked on a mattress for the little bed

March 9 cleaned and scalded my bed

16 Milla sick – Dr Shelburne to attend her – Mary Eleanor born

1867

March 31 This week pieced Aunt Ann a quilt - want to go to Mrs Leech to help her get out her quilt

1868

March 10 The past week I carded rolls for 6 cuts of cotton – wove 10 yds of cloth and put in Aunt Ann's quilt and quilted 2 days

April 5 quilted a lincy quilt for Tobe wove 6 ½ yards table cloth – made Mr Carpenter a shirt – pieced some on my Lounge quilt

April 20 This week I Wove 10 yds and got out my pieces of table cloths and made one – finished piecing my lounge quilt

April 26 I quilted my lounge quilt with help and made Aunt Ann an apron and Tobe a pair of draws

September 6 Spent some hours this morning helping to pink the trimming for Mrs Julia Russels coffin – she has gone from this earth after only a few days illness – she leaves a young infant

September 28 Two weeks has passed since I have noted anything on thy fair pages – a merciful Providence has still blessed us with all things necessary for our comforts – I do feel very thankful for the same – the first of two weeks the men were herding cattle – they left on Saturday the 12th – they have gone to Kansas with them – made Alvin Clark a pair of drawers and a roundabout coat – Gippy a shirt – Anna a dress and fixed and quilted a comfort and bound it – patched as usual

1869

January In this month I have been sick most of the time (Benjamin was born New Year's Eve) but will set down what little I did, pieced 3 old quilts – one for Aunt Ann and one for the Lounge and one for the little bed.

1870

July 19 Some travelers stopped to stay all night and one of them got sick which hindered me some

1874

February 3 I worked on a new quilt for Martha our hired girl

4 I cooked dinner today as Martha was washing

5 I made a cap for Bennie to day and finished setting a quilt together for Martha

July 25 Milla and Annie, once our servants, came to see us to day – I was glad to see them.

1876

March 17 Adelia Brown brought the quilt squares she had been piecing for me – her horse got loose and she had to walk home.

1878

May 1 Yesterday got dinner and batted some cotton and put in a lounge quilt and quilted some – I want to quilt a goodeal to day – so I must get at it.

October 21 have quilted a calico comfort – Martha is washing to day and I have been busy and not much settled work – been mending some – a made a little grape wine – got dinner and now I must get at something

1880

October 19 I have put in a comfort and quilted it tolerably close.

A Quilt for the Help

PIECED BY BETSY CHUTCHIAN AND FRIENDS
QUILTED BY SHERI MECOM
48" x 72"

A Quilt for the Help could have been meant for any number of servants in the Carpenter household over the years. Milla, Jane, Aunt Ann, Martha and more were all recipients of Lizzie's quilts. Hired hands and boarders came and went and needed cover and comfort, as well.

Fabrics

2 ¾ yards total assorted dark prints, stripes and plaids
2 yards total assorted light and medium prints, stripes and plaids
½ yard for binding
3 ¼ yards backing (with crosswise seam) or 4 ½ yards (with lengthwise seam)

Cutting

From light and medium fabrics, cut:
200 – 3" squares for pinwheel blocks
36 – 5" squares for half-square triangle blocks

From dark fabrics, cut:
200 – 3" squares for pinwheel blocks
36 – 5" squares for half-square triangle blocks
44 – 4 ½" squares for alternate blocks

Block assembly
Pinwheel Block

4" finished

1. Pair contrasting 3" squares, right sides together, draw a diagonal line from corner to corner on the back of the lightest square and stitch ¼" on each side of the drawn line.

2. Cut unit apart on drawn line. Press to dark. Trim each unit to 2 ½".

3. Select 4 triangle units to make pinwheel block, stitch as shown.

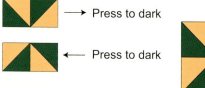 → Press to dark

← Press to dark

Make 100

Note: The pinwheels may spin to left or right.

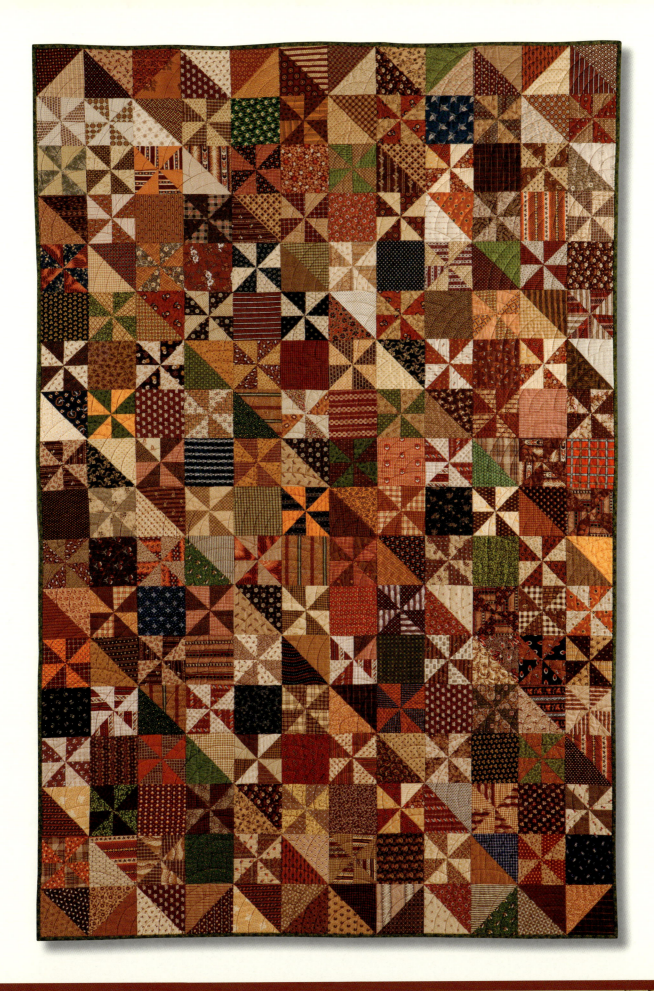

Half square block

1. Pair contrasting 5" squares and sew in same manner as for pinwheel blocks. Cut apart on drawn line. Press to darker triangle. Trim unit to 4 ½".

Make 72

From the constructed blocks, make the following larger blocks:

1. Arrange 4 pinwheel blocks and sew together as shown.
   Make 2

2. Arrange 2 half-square blocks and 2 pinwheel blocks and sew together as shown.
   Make 24

3. Arrange 2 alternate squares and 2 pinwheel blocks and sew together as shown.
   Make 22

4. Referring to the assembly diagram below, make 2 rows of 12 blocks with the remaining half-square triangle units for the top and bottom of the quilt.

Quilt top assembly

Arrange the blocks as shown in quilt diagram. Sew in rows then join rows.

Finishing

A Quilt for the Help is machine quilted in a *Baptist Fan* design. A simple finish for a very scrappy utility quilt – made for warmth and comfort. Bind in a fabric of your choice.

Assembly Diagram

Quilt for Milla's Babe

Quilt for Milla's Babe

PIECED AND HAND QUILTED BY BETSY CHUTCHIAN
40" x 48"
8" FINISHED BLOCK
20 BLOCKS

Milla, one of the Carpenter's slaves and Lizzie were pregnant at the same time. Milla gave birth to Mary Eleanor in March 1861 and Lizzie gave birth to Jeff, my great grandfather in April. That Winter and Spring, Lizzie was quite busy making cradle quilts, quilts for the little bed and quilts for the help as well as helping others quilt. I had extra triangles after making *A Quilt for the Help*, perfect for using in the *Quilt for Milla's Babe*. This is something Lizzie would have done. You may wish to make extra triangles, as well, to have handy for another quilt.

Fabric Requirements

¾ yard light to medium prints for blocks
¾ yard medium to dark prints for blocks
(Or 1 ½ yard total assorted light, medium and dark prints)
⅔ yard total of 2 different prints for borders
1 ½ yards for backing
⅓ yard for binding

Cutting

From the block prints, cut: 80 – 5" squares

From the border prints, cut 4 – 4 ½" x 40 ½" strips of 2 fabrics

From the binding fabric, cut 5 – 2 ¼" x the width of fabric strips

Block Assembly

1. Pair 2 contrasting squares, right sides together. Draw a diagonal line, corner to corner and stitch ¼" on each side of the drawn line. Make 40 pairs.

2. Cut apart on drawn line and press to the dark. Trim each unit to 4 ½" square. Make 80 units.

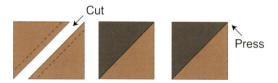

3. Arrange 4 triangle units as shown in the diagram to make a Broken Dishes block. Make 20 – 8" finished blocks.

Press ⟶

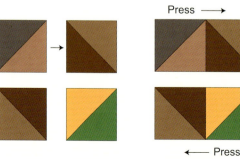

⟵ Press

Make 20

Quilt Top Assembly

1. Arrange 5 rows of 4 blocks. Stitch rows together, then join rows. The top center should measure 32 ½" x 40 ½".

2. Stitch 2 border strips to sides. Press to the border. Sew 2 strips to top and bottom. Press.

Finishing

Quilt as desired. I hand quilted a Baptist Fan using a utility stitch and perle cotton. Bind with fabric of your choice.

Assembly Diagram

Lounge Quilt

PIECED BY BETSY CHUTCHIAN AND SONJA KRAUS
QUILTED BY SHERI MECOM

71" X 84 ¹/₂"
BLOCK SIZE 9 ¹/₂" FINISHED

One category of quilts Lizzie made was lounge quilts. Lizzie would write that she made a quilt for the lounge or made a lounge quilt. Did the Carpenter home have a room called the lounge or was there a piece of furniture called a lounge? Whether for a room or furniture, quilts for the lounge meant quilts for overnight guests. Guests were always welcome and comforted – friends, family or strangers.

Fabrics
For Blocks

2 ½ yards total assorted light, medium, and dark prints for 4 patches and half-square triangle units
⅛ yard red for center square
⅔ yard blue for block sashing
3 ½" yards pink print for setting squares and triangles
½ yard for 2 ¼" double fold binding

Cutting

From the assorted prints, cut:
320 – 2 ½" squares of light medium and dark
56 – 3 ¼" squares of medium and dark
56 – 3 ¼" squares of light

From the blue print, cut:
80 – 2" x 4 ½" rectangles

From the red print, cut:
20 – 2" squares

From pink print, cut:
4 – 14 ¾" squares – cut each twice on the diagonal
2 – 7 ⅝" squares – cut each once on the diagonal
12 – 10" squares
8 – 6 ½" x the width of fabric strips

From the binding print, cut:
8 – 2 ¼" x the width of fabric strips

Block Assembly

1. Make 4 four-patch units from 2 light or medium squares and 2 dark squares as shown.

2. Sew 2 sashes to four-patch units as shown. Press to sashing.

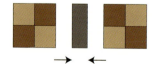

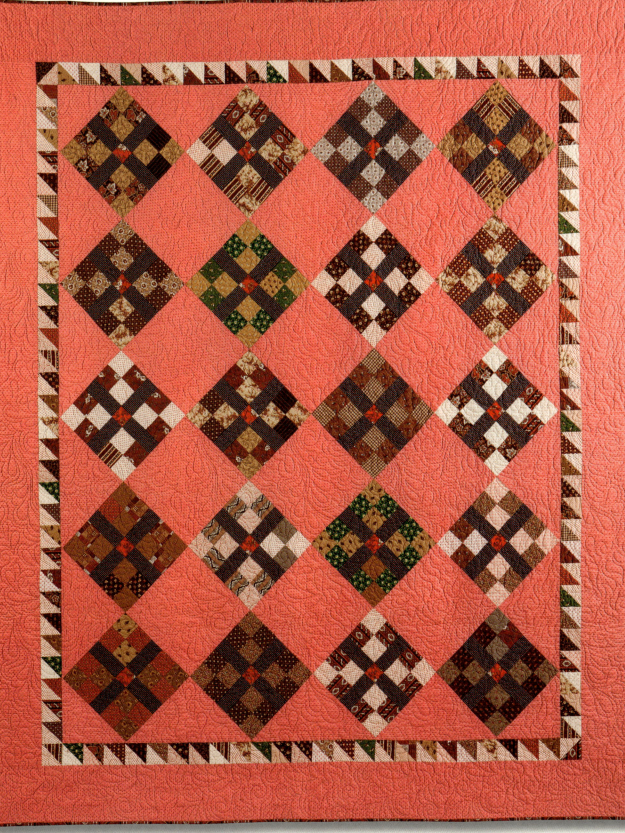

3. Sew 2 sashes to center square. Press to sash.

4. Join pieced sash to units made in Step 2.

Make 20 blocks

2. Referring to the quilt assembly diagram, sew 2 strips of 30 triangle units together. Stitch to sides of quilt top. Sew 2 strips of 26 triangles units together to the top and bottom of the quilt.

3. Add outer border strips: Measure quilt lengthwise through center, piece border strips to match that measurement. Stitch to sides. Measure quilt crosswise through center, piece border strips to match that measurement. Stitch to the top and bottom.

Finishing

The Lounge Quilt is machine quilted in an allover pattern. Bind in fabric of your choice.

Quilt Top Assembly

Arrange the blocks, setting squares, setting triangles and corners in diagonal rows as shown in the assembly diagram. Stitch rows together. Press to setting pieces. The quilt top should now measure 54 ½" x 68".

Borders

1. Sew the half-square triangle units: Pair 56 – 3 ¼" squares of light prints and 56 – 3 ¼" squares of medium and dark prints right sides together. Draw a diagonal line and stitch ¼" on each side of drawn line. Cut apart on drawn line, pressing to darker print. Trim unit to 2 ¾" square.

Make 112 units

Assembly Diagram

CHAPTER 4

Grasshoppers, Flies and Fleas, Butterflies and Bees

Insects, most often a destructive force on the farm, tormented animals and humans alike, ruined crops and devastated a farmer's livelihood. Grasshoppers arrived twice a year, Spring and Fall, and could eat up new growth over night, forcing crops to be replanted, if and when the weather cooperated. Flies tormented animals and fleas plagued the household in late Spring and Summer. Bees swarmed frequently and stung at will but the reward was honey. Certain butterflies were pests too; Lizzie called them skippers.

Battling the pests was a seasonal concern with economic repercussions. The loss of any crop could be quite costly when the family was dependent upon its success. A farmer's patience, and his family's, could certainly be tested until the pests wrecked havoc and left.

1862

May 10 Scoured and scalded the beds – the bees swarmed this morning – I helped hive them - patched some in the evening

29 Made Jane a dress and hived a swarm of bees

21 Made Jane an underwaist and Ann dress – bees swarmed again – got John Brown to help me

1868

April 5 My garden looks well and I will soon have plenty of vegetables if the grass hoppers only would leave it alone – there are a great number of them very small but they already commenced to destroy some things.

1870

May 19 As it has been more than a week since I wrote any in my book I thought I would pen a few items to night - but can't say much on account of the fleas, they are eating me dreadful, we have a good supply this spring as usual – Ma and Mary Ann and Aronia all came and spent the day with me – I had green bean and Irish potatoes. The first of the season – I will quit - Oh the fleas

July 5 A few items to night and I expect to say only a few things for the fleas are pestering me very badly – the thresher came to thresh our wheat – I want to go see Owen – he has been sick but can't because the thresher is here - will quit for the night – Oh the fleas

1872

June 11 Can't write the fleas bite me so

1874

July 29 Scalded the beds in the dining room – found a good many bugs – scoured the floor

November 5 To day I fixed away the honey and squeezed out some - set me some vinegar to sour

1876

March 22 Some men here this evening with a patent bee hive – we are having a hive transferred and some honey taken out – the gentlemen remained all night

June 26 This evening Mr C took some honey. He got a right smart honey and several stings.

September 21 The hoppers are very numerous indeed – eating up most every green and tender plant and herb

1877

March 13 Our boys finished sowing oats today – Mr C and some of them made some garden down in the field, as the grasshoppers are too numerous to plant in our garden here at the house – they are hatching out very briskly – I expect they will play havoc with the young vegetation.

March 21 In the morning I made some sacks to sack the bacon hams to keep out the skippers

May 1 The grasshoppers are eating the corn and wheat so that it looks like tis hardly worthwhile to plant or plow - I'm working on a pair of pillow slips – ornamental ones.

May 10 My babe is not quite well of her cough but is so much better I ventured to take her to her grandma's and left while I went to Plano, did not stay long – was gone just 3 hours – got some yards to make some clothes for the boys for summer. People are not buying much at present on account the grass hoppers are eating some things up.

May 26 The hoppers have been numerous - but are gone now thanks be to the Lord

1880

June 15 Late in the evening Mr Carpenter rode down in the field to look at the crops – found things looked well except the cotton the worms ate up – looks like the rain will ensure a good corn crop – Willie and Johnie have been cutting oats here – Mr Chandler and Old Uncle John are stacking wheat – (all) hindered by rain

July 21 Mr Allen helped the boys take some honey and got several bee stings as well as the rest. They got a goodeal of honey. I have been quite busy today making some jelly and preserves and putting away honey and cleaning up and cooking, etc so I have not got much quilting done today.

August 12 this evening the clouds grew blacker and blacker … I fear they won't get their grain covered so as to keep dry – I expect this will finish the threshing here – the flies are so bad they almost kill the stock – they will have to quit on that account and wait until the weather gets cooler or the flies die out or leave

September 10 Mr Carpenter is now busied gathering up his cattle that has been scattered by the flies

Shoo!

PIECED BY BETSY CHUTCHIAN
QUILTED BY SHERI MECOM

56" x 66 ½"

9" FINISHED BLOCK

Bugs – being inundated by bugs of all sorts – were an ongoing problem that Lizzie reported in a recurring manner throughout the years. A shoo-fly variation block multiplied by many seems the perfect quilt to represent the wrath caused by insects. Whether by annoyance or destruction, insects were an integral part of farm life. Shoo!

Fabrics

2 yards total assorted cream to light tan prints (A) (B)
1 ¼ yards total assorted brown and purple prints (C) (D)
⅛ yard purple print (F)
1 ½ yards green print for sash (E) and the first and third borders
⅞ yard medium black print for sashing
½ yard purple print for the second border
⅔ yard black print for cornerstones and binding
4 yards for the backing

Cutting

From the assorted cream prints, cut:
160 – 2 ½" squares for the half-square triangles (A)
320 – 1 ½" x 2" rectangles (B)

From the assorted brown and purple prints, cut:
160 – 2 ½" squares for the half-square triangles (C)
80 – 1 ½" squares (D)

From green print, cut:
80 – 1 ½" x 4 ½" rectangles (E)
12 – 2 ½" x the width of fabric strips for the first and third borders

From small amount of purple print, cut:
20 – 1 ½" x 1 ½" squares (F)

From second purple print, cut:
6 – 2 ½" strips selvage to selvage for the second border

From medium black print, cut:
49 – 2" x 9 ½" strips

From black prints, cut:
30 – 2" x 2" squares
7 – 2 ¼" x the width of fabric strips for double fold binding

Block Assembly

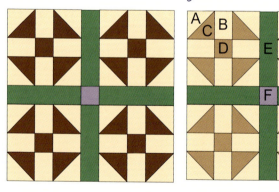

1. Make half-square triangle units by pairing 8 light squares (A) and 8 dark squares (C). Draw a diagonal line on wrong side of light print. Stitch ¼" away on each side of drawn line. Cut apart on drawn line.
Press to dark print.
Trim to 2" square.

2. Make 4 Shoo-fly variation blocks by joining units as shown with 4 (B) rectangles.

→ ← Press

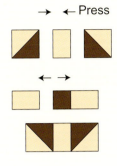

Make 4

3. Join the blocks with sash and cornerstone.

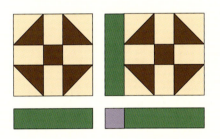

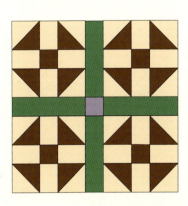

Make 20 blocks

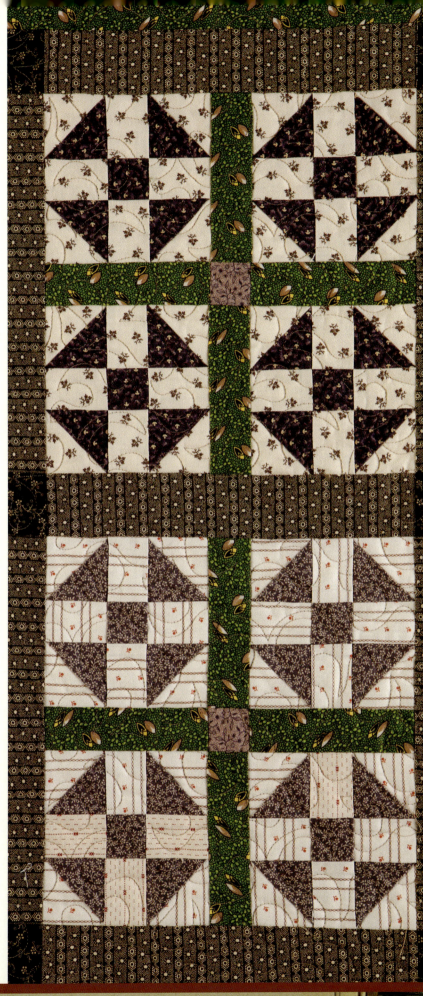

Quilt Assembly

Referring to the quilt diagram, join blocks and sashing.

1. Join 5 black cornerstones to 4 medium black sashing strips.

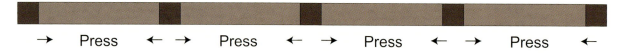

→ Press ← → Press ← → Press ← → Press ←

Make 6 pieced sashing sets

2. Join 5 sashing strips to 4 blocks.

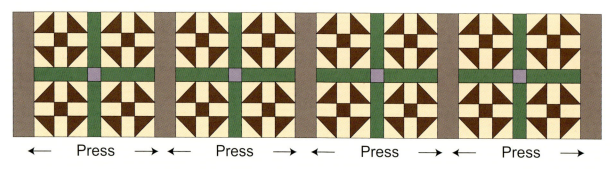

← Press → ← Press → ← Press → ← Press →

Make 5 rows

3. Sew rows of sashing and rows of blocks together. The top should measure 44" x 54 ½".

Borders

4. Following the quilt diagram, add borders (strips pieced to match measurements given). Always start with side border strips, then add top and bottom strips.

   Piece strips to match measurements given:
   First border green: 2 – 2 ½" x 54 ½" for the sides and 2 – 2 ½" x 48" for the top and bottom.
   Second border purple: 2 – 2 ½" x 58 ½" for the sides and 2 – 2 ½" x 52" for the top and bottom.
   Third border green: 2 – 2 ½" x 62 ½" for the sides and 2 – 2 ½" x 56" for the top and bottom.

Finishing

Shoo! is quilted in an allover paisley design with a black, double fold binding.

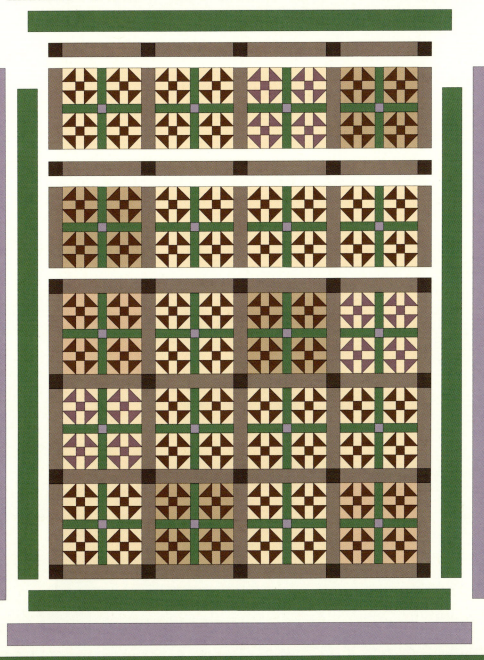

Assembly Diagram

Honey Bee Pincushion

MADE BY BETTY EDGELL

Block size 6"

Bees, so necessary for pollination of fruits and vegetables, played a very important role in farm life. While most insects on the farm offered nothing helpful, the function of bees was quite the contrary. Bees play an important role in the pollination of blooms for fruits and vegetables, insuring a bountiful harvest for the Carpenter table. Lizzie planted quite a variety of vegetables in her garden and gathered peaches from the prairie's edge. Bees were hived when they swarmed. Lizzie wrote of bees stinging Robert and others, but never her, when gathering their honey. Besides a sweet treat for the table, honey provided another source of income.

Fabrics

Small amounts of: dark green gold and small plaid felted wool
7" square flannel backing
1 skein gold embroidery floss
Crushed walnut shells for filling pincushion (found at pet stores and some quilt shops)

Cutting

From the gold, cut:
5 – 1 ½" squares

From the plaid, cut:
4 – 1 ½" squares

From the dark green, cut:
2 – 2" x 3 ½" rectangles
2 – 2" x 6 ½" rectangles

Using template A,
cut 4 gold bee body shapes.
Using template B,
cut 8 gold wing shapes.

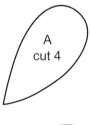

Block Assembly

1. Using a generous ¼" seam, sew a nine-patch block of five gold squares and 4 plaid squares. Press seams open to reduce bulk.

2. Add side rectangles, then top and bottom rectangles. Press to the rectangles.

3. Following the diagram for placement, appliqué shapes to pieced block using a whip stitch with one or 2 strands of floss.

Finishing

With right sides together, sew the wool top to the flannel back, wool side up, sew with a generous ¼" seam all around, leaving a 2" opening. Fill with crushed walnut shells. Stitch opening closed.

CHAPTER 5

Passing Time

Free time was a luxury in the Carpenter household and on the farm. With a strict schedule established to keep house and farm running well and maintain productivity, time away from the daily routine of work and chores was a cooperative effort. Leisure time was spent in a variety of ways. For Lizzie it could be going to or hosting quilting parties, a ride on the prairie, visiting with friends and family over dinner after Sunday meeting, spending day in town and grabbing a few moments to write in her dear journal. For the boys, hunting, fishing, trapping birds, or playing games would provide a welcome break from chores. In the Spring of 1880, Robert took Lizzie back to Kentucky for a few weeks to visit family and friends. Passing time by any means different from the normal routine offered a healthy and much needed change of pace.

1858

March 13   Went to Ma's in the evening to help sis on her quilt - sewed a little - went fishing

1866

January 8   Mr Carpenter and Dick Clark netting birds – caught a fine chance

June 3   Today is the warmest of the season – When it gets cool this evening I want to ride out on the on the prairie – I'm tired of sitting around the house

1867

March 28   I've been to Mrs Leeches to day to a quilting - there was a good many persons there – eight married women ladies and nine or ten young girls – we did not get a great deal quilted, rolled twice – it was a new quilt of Miss Emily's

31   Just returned from a short walk down in the pararie to see Ball's colt or little mule rather which has just come to this part of the country

1874

June 29   Monday, it did not rain as some expected – to day I hemed six towels and two sheets and made Eddy a dress, in the evening I went up to Ma's to help her on her quilt – Mrs Bush and Lora and Miss Pickens came just as I got there and after staying a little while we all came down here where the ladies took a game at Croquet.

July 4   This morning I cleaned up the house above stairs and below mended some half dozen garments – some five or six girls here to day, or this evening to play croquet – had a high time I recon – at least they all seemed very fond of the sport.

October 6 Mr Carpenter, myself and Johny and Eddie went to the fair to day – we had a very pleasant time there – not a great many persons present but the articles exhibited were many and pretty good

9 Mr Carpenter, myself and the little boys went to the fair to day – This is the first time I ever went when the horses were showed and I liked very much to see them ride

1876

January 14 I worked this morning on a quilt for the little bed and in the evening worked on a quilt I will call Eddie's a worsted log cabin

1877

May 30 No company for Sunday dinner - In the evening I rode out on the pararie to try my new saddle Mr C bought me last week in Dallas

1878

July 4 Gip and John took their base ball suit and expected to play a match game with the Plano B-Ball club – I have been working on a quilt and just finished sweeping the house for it is mudy.

20 want to make some peach butter – also some light bread and sweep and clean up which is my Saturday work especially – the boys have gone to Plano this eve to play base ball with the Plano Club – the little boys have been gathering peaches

May 1 Mr C – myself and little boys went to McKinney Saturday – on the train – the boys had not riden on the cars before – we came back in the wagon with Willie and Emma

1879

May 1 Pic Nic at Bethany with music and Tournament Riding - Jimmie Mathews taking 1st crown and the white rock boys taking the next two – glad it is over for I do think tournament riding is a dangerous business.

1880

February 8 Made 4 articles this week and worked some on Eddie's quilt

11 This evening I have a bonnet on hand to finish for Vina Taylor and several quilts I take a few stitches in now and then

19 Yesterday I finished Jeff's quilt or the one intended for him – called the plated hexagon – I also worked some on the one Eddie claims - a worsted one called bird trap.

March 14 Two years ago our dear babe Mary Katie was buried - I will go up to her little grave and take some flowers – I have been working on Eddie's quilt this week

15 Finished Eddie's quilt to day (bird trap)

April 20 My good journal as I have been busied have neglected to tell you anything for some days – but must not do so longer – although I am quite busy now – Mr Carpenter and myself are talking of starting on a trip to Kentucky Monday the 26th of this month – expect to be gone about 3 weeks. Cousin Sue Shelburn is talking of going with us – hope we may have a pleasant trip and safe return to our good home again in Texas.

June 1 Lizzie wrote extensively of the trip to Kentucky, how sick she was on the train, but no details of the two weeks there except to report, "We had a pleasant time so much so that it will always me a green spot in my memory."

August 8 I sewed some Monday and Tuesday and helped scour and clean up – In the evening I started cooking for a little quilting and Croquet party on Wednesday eve – there were not many persons but I was glad to see those that did come – They seemed to enjoy themselves tolerably well

November 6 Mr Davis and the little boys are gone hunting rabbits – as tis a fine morning for that – some ice on the rainbarrel about an inch thick – at sunrise mercury stood at 24.

1882

May 18 All well with us to day – Mr Carpenter is plowing to day and Bennie and Eddie are hoeing, all in the corn – Jeffie is helping Mr Davis in there cotton to day – Gippie and Bobbie have gone on Elm to hunt and fish a day or two

Croquet

MADE AND QUILTED BY BETSY CHUTCHIAN
35 ³/₄" x 41 ³/₄"
5 ¹/₄" FINISHED BLOCK

During the late 1860's through the early 1880's, croquet was a very popular lawn game in the United States. Women especially enjoyed the game. Hosting a game of croquet offered a nice opportunity for Lizzie to entertain young ladies – a pleasant change from the comings and goings of all the boys and their friends.

Fabrics

¾ yard cream
2 yards cheddar
1 ¼ yards for backing
¼ yard for a single fold binding

Note: Prewash fabrics, press well and starch. When working with strips, especially narrow ones, I prefer pressing with starch. The strips cut cleaner, and after sewing each step, press better. This helps to prevent distortion.

Cutting and Strip Sets Construction

To make the croquet block, you'll need a center nine-patch and two rounds of strips surrounding it. The quilt is set together with pieced sashing.

Nine-patch unit

For the nine-patch unit, cut:
5 cream strips 1 ¼" x the width of fabric
4 cheddar strips 1 ¼" x the width of fabric

Strip Set A
1. Sew 2 cream strips to either side of 1 cheddar strip. Press to the dark. The pieced unit will be 2 ¾" wide. Make 2 sets.

2. Sub cut at 1 ¼" intervals. Cut 60.

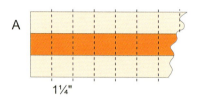

A   1¼"

Strip Set B
1. Sew 2 cheddar strips to either side of 1 cream strip. Press to the dark. The pieced unit will be 2 ¾" wide. Make 1 set.
2. Sub cut at 1 ¼" intervals. Cut 30.

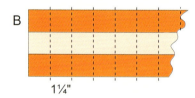

B   1¼"

Round 1

For round 1, cut:
4 cheddar strips 2 ¾" x the width of fabric
4 cream strips 1 ¼" x the width of fabric

Set C
1. Sub cut 2 of the cheddar strips at 1 ¼" intervals. Cut 60.

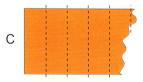

C

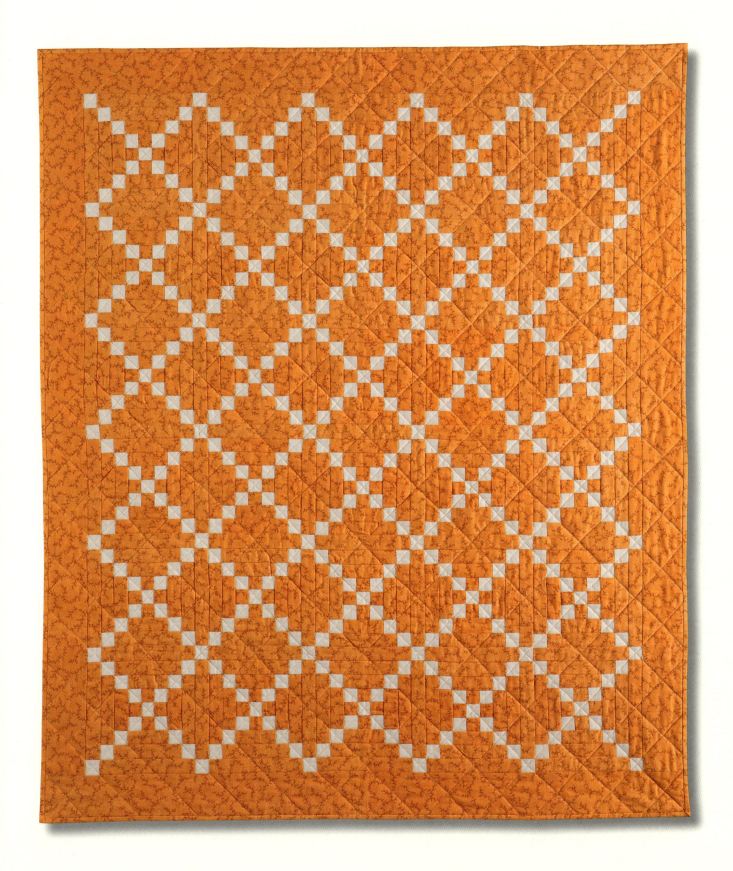

Strip Set D

1. Sew 2 cream strips to either side of 1 cheddar strip. Press to the dark. The pieced unit will be 4 ¼" wide. Make 2 sets.
2. Sub cut at 1 ¼" intervals. Cut 60.

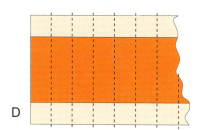

Round 2

For round 2, cut:

Cut 4 cheddar strips 4 ¼" x the width of fabric

Cut 4 cream strips 1 ¼" x the width of fabric

Set E

1. Sub cut 2 of the cheddar strips at 1 ¼" intervals. Cut 60.

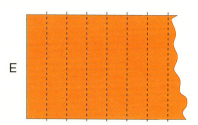

Strip Set F

1. Sew 2 cream strips to either side of 1 cheddar strip. Press to the dark. The pieced unit will be 5 ¾" wide. Make 2 sets.
2. Sub cut at 1 ¼" intervals. Cut 60.

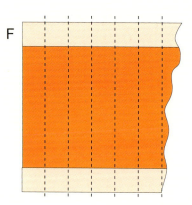

Sashing

For the sashing, cut:

3 cheddar strips 5 ¾" x the width of fabric

2 cream strips 1 ¼" x the width of fabric

Set G

1. Sub cut the 3 cheddar strips at 1 ¼" intervals. Cut 71.

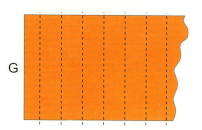

Set H

1. Sub cut the 2 cream strips into 1 ¼" x 1 ¼" squares for the cornerstones. Cut 42.

Block Assembly

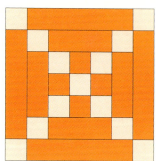

1. Assemble the center nine-patch unit by sewing 2 Strip Set A units to either side of 1 Strip Set B unit. Press to one side. This unit measures 2 ¾". Make 30.

A   B   A

2. Add round 1 by sewing 2 Set C strips to either side of the nine-patch unit. Press to the strip.

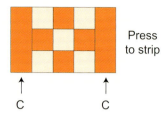

Press to strip

C   C

3. Sew 2 Strip Set D units to the top and bottom. Press to the strip. The unit measures 4 ¼".

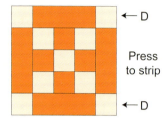

← D

Press to strip

← D

4. Add round 2 by sewing 2 Set E strips to either side of the block. Press to the strip.

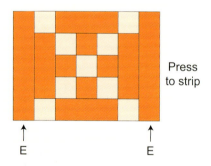

Press to strip

E   E

5. To finish the block, sew 2 Strip Set F units to the top and bottom. Press to the strip. The block measures 5 ¾".

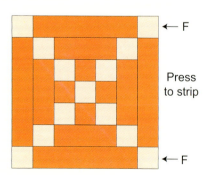

← F

Press to strip

← F

Quilt Top

1. Lay out 5 blocks alternating with 6 Set G sashing strips. Sew together referring to the diagram for placement. Press to the sashing. Make 6 rows.

2. Lay out 5 Set G sashing strips alternating with 6 Set H cornerstones. Sew together referring to the diagram for placement. Press to Set G strips. Make 7 rows.

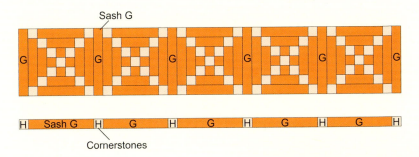

3. Join sashing rows alternating with the block rows according to the assembly diagram. The top should measure 31 ¼" x 37 ¼".

Borders

From the cheddar, cut:
2 – 2 ¾" x 37 ¼" for the sides
2 – 2 ¾" x 35 ¾" for the top and bottom

1. Sew the side strips on first and press to the border.

2. Sew the top and bottom next to finish the top.
   Press to the border.

Finishing

Croquet is simply quilted in a diagonal grid following the lines of the blocks. Bind with a single fold binding in cheddar from strips cut 1 ⅛".

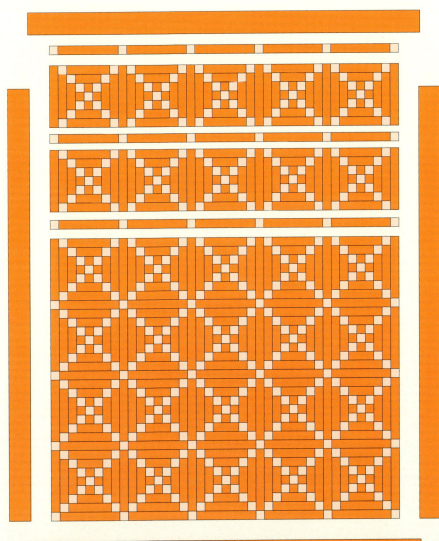

Assembly Diagram

Bird Trap

The Bird Trap Mystery

Before recreating a Log Cabin quilt Lizzie wrote about making, I was fascinated by the words her son Eddie used to describe the quilt: bird trap. Puzzled by the comparison, I searched references for log cabin blocks and variations to see if some variation was indeed called a Bird Trap. After finding no reference to the name I determined it was just that, a name given to that particular Log Cabin quilt by her son.

In 2010, a conversation with my dad over dinner one evening solved the mystery. Dad was 91 at the time and I casually asked if he knew what a bird trap was. His answer was short and precise.

"Yes, but it was never very successful."

Successful or not, was not the point of my question, so I asked if he ever built one.

"Yes I have," he said.

"Daddy can you draw me a picture of it?" I asked.

This is what he drew:

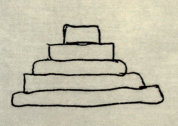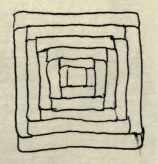

The two pictures are clearly a courthouse steps block! Dad drew logs starting with the outside, to represent pieces of wood slats larger on the outside, with progressively smaller pieces over lapping at corners until the pyramid shape was completed, leaving a small square opening in the center. He told me, he would then "prop up one side with a stick and put a little food or bread crumbs inside to lure in the bird. The bird would either knock down the wood slats by flapping wings or the stick could be pulled and the wood would fall."

But as Daddy said, "it was never very successful." I then saw what Eddie saw, and for me ... it was success.

MADE BY BETSY CHUTCHIAN
34 ¹/₄" x 47 ³/₄"
35 – 6 ³/₄" FINISHED BLOCKS

For my *Bird Trap* quilt, I chose to use a foundation piecing method, the same as used in the antique quilt, so I would have a finished quilt at the end of piecing. If you don't want to make your quilt this way, use the cutting and block assembly instructions to piece your blocks traditionally. Then layer with batting and backing and quilt as desired to finish.

Fabrics

⅛ yard red for center of block (A)
⅛ yard yellow for center of block (B)
2 yards total assorted light prints
2 yards assorted dark prints
35 – 9" x 9" squares of assorted medium and dark prints for foundation pieced backing
¼ yard for 1 ⅛" single fold binding

Additional supplies

Fine permanent pen

Cutting

Note: Pre-wash and press all fabric with starch before cutting.

Block A

From red print for center square, cut:

18 – 1 ¼" x 1 ¼" squares

From assorted light prints, cut:

36 – 1 ¼" x 1 ¼" squares
36 – 1 ¼" x 2 ¾" rectangles
36 – 1 ¼" x 4 ¼" rectangles
36 – 1 ¼" x 5 ¾" rectangles

From assorted dark prints, cut:

36 – 1 ¼" x 2 ¾" rectangles

36 – 1 ¼" x 4 ¼" rectangles

36 – 1 ¼" x 5 ¾" rectangles

36 – 1 ¼" x 7 ¼" rectangles

Block B

From yellow print for center square, cut:

17 – 1 ¼" x 1 ¼" squares

From assorted light prints, cut:

34 – 1 ¼" x 2 ¾" rectangles

34 – 1 ¼" x 4 ¼" rectangles

34 – 1 ¼" x 5 ¾" rectangles

34 – 1 ¼" x 7 ¼" rectangles

From assorted dark prints, cut:

34 – 1 ¼" x 1 ¼" squares

34 – 1 ¼" x 2 ¾" rectangles

34 – 1 ¼" x 4 ¼" rectangles

34 – 1 ¼" x 5 ¾" rectangles

For 1 ⅛" single fold binding, cut:

4 – 1 ⅛" strips x the width of fabric

Foundation Backings

Pre-wash, press and starch the 35 – 9" x 9" assorted medium and dark foundation backing squares before cutting. Starch the squares until they are stiff. This will help when piecing the blocks. After they are starched, cut the squares into 35 – 8" x 8" squares.

Block Assembly for Foundation Piecing

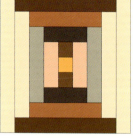

The block assembly for foundation piecing method will result in a "quilt as you go" block. Once these blocks are joined together, the entire quilt is finished – no additional quilting is needed. There is no batting so the weight of the quilt is lighter, what is often called a summer spread.

1. On each 8" square, draw diagonal lines in an X from corner to corner on the wrong side of the fabric, using a fine permanent pen.

Make 35

2. Place all 35 squares, right side up in a pleasing arrangement on a design board in 7 rows of 5 blocks each. Next, keeping each square in place turn over so wrong side is facing up. Mark each square 1-35 in the upper left hand corner and mark (A) and (B) alternately on each block. By pre-arranging the foundation squares, you can control color placement.

1 A	2 B	3 A	4 B	5 A
6 B	7 A	8 B	9 A	10 B
11 A	12 B	13 A	14 B	15 A
16 B	17 A	18 B	19 A	20 B
21 A	22 B	23 A	24 B	25 A
26 B	27 A	28 B	29 A	30 B
31 A	32 B	33 A	34 B	35 A

Arrangement of A and B Blocks

Block A Assembly

1. Place a red center square on the center of the foundation square. Use the X to align the square exactly in the center.

Round 1:

1. On the opposite sides of the center, add sew 2 – 1 ¼" x 1 ¼" light squares. Start stitching ¼" from edge, back-stitch, stop ¼" from end and backstitch. Do this each time you add pieces.
Press to the light.

2. Next, sew 2 – 1 ¼" x 2 ¾" dark rectangles to the top and bottom. Press to dark. Note that corners align with the drawn lines on foundation.

Round 2:

1. Sew 2- 1 ¼" x 2 ¾" light rectangles, press to light. Then sew 2 – 1 ¼" x 4 ¼" dark rectangles, press to dark.

Round 3:

1. Sew 2 – 1 ¼" x 4 ¼" light rectangles, press to light. Then sew 2 – 1 ½" x 5 ¾" dark rectangles press to dark.

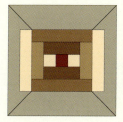 

Round 4:

1. Sew 2 – 1 ¼" x 5 ¾" light rectangles, press to light. Then sew 2 – 1 ¼" x 7 ¼" dark rectangles. Start and stop stitching the last rectangles ½" away from edges and back stitch. Press to the dark.

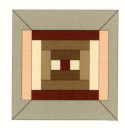 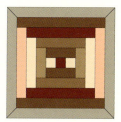

Block B Assembly

For the B blocks, repeat the process as follows, starting and stopping seams ¼" from edges and backstitching.

1. Place a yellow center square on the center of the foundation square. Use the X to align the square exactly in the center.

Round 1:

1. Sew: 2 – 1 ¼" x 1 ¼" dark squares to each side of the center square. Press to the dark. Then sew 2 – 1 ¼" x 2 ¾" light rectangles. Press to the light.

Round 2:

1. Sew: 2 – 1 ¼" x 2 ¾" dark rectangles, press to dark. Then sew 2 – 1 ¼" x 4 ¼" light rectangles. Press to light.

Round 3:

1. Sew 2 – 1 ¼" x 4 ¼"" dark rectangles, press to the dark. Then sew 2 – 1 ¼" x 5 ¾" light rectangles. Press to the light.

Round 4:

1. Sew 2 – 1 ¼" x 5 ¾" dark rectangles, press to the dark. Then sew 2 – 1 ¼" x 7 ¼" light rectangles, press to the light.

Quilt Top Assembly

1. Place blocks in order following diagram on page 82.

2. Starting with blocks 1-5 in row 1, stitch the blocks right sides together through 3 layers leaving foundations of Block B free, pinning away from the stitching. Use a ¼" seam, matching blocks together. The foundations of each block may be trimmed as need when you are ready to hand stitch. Press to Block B. Stop and start with backstitch ¼" from edge. Add each block to the previously sewn blocks. Press to Block B.

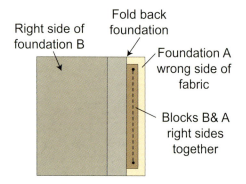

Right side of foundation B

Fold back foundation

Foundation A wrong side of fabric

Blocks B& A right sides together

3. Stitch blocks 6-10 in row 2, in similar manner, pressing to the B blocks, leaving the foundations (B) free. Add each block to the previously sewn blocks.

4. Repeat the process for each row.

5. From the backside of the row, hand stitch the foundation (B) by folding the foundation fabric over the sewn seam of Block A even with the machine stitching, trimming foundation (A) as needed once you are ready to hand stitch the seam closed. Repeat process in each row.

6. Join the rows starting with rows 1 and 2. Keep one side of foundation free, stitching through 3 layers, with the pieced block and foundations of the row against the feed dogs. You may trim the stitched foundation edge even with blocks after stitching. Hand stitch the free edge of the row even with seam.

7. Repeat process, adding next row in order, and stitching before adding next row.

Finishing

Once all rows are joined, you have a quilted top. *Bird Trap* has a narrow single fold binding.

Note: If you prefer to make this quilt in the traditional method, use the cutting and block assembly instructions to piece your blocks. Follow quilt assembly diagram below to assemble the quilt top. Then layer with batting and backing and quilt as desired to finish.

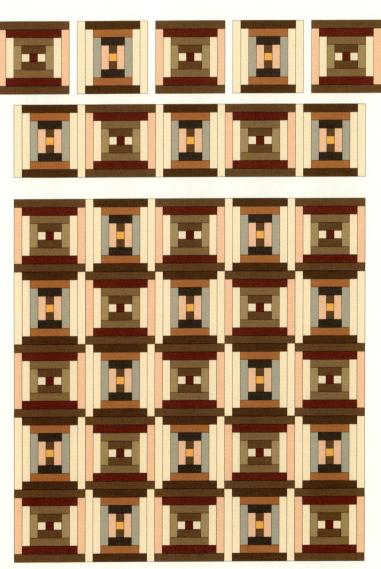

Assembly Diagram

Lizzie, Eddie and Mary Katie, 1877

Lizzie's youngest son Eddie, upon graduation from Pharmacy school in Philadelphia.

Elizabeth Ann Mathews Carpenter

Born October 12, 1832
Oldham County, Kentucky
Died September 24, 1882
Plano, Collin County, Texas

From Lizzie's obituary: "Blessed are the dead who die in the Lord henceforth, yes saith the Spirit; that they may rest from their labors, for their works do follow them." Rev. xiv 13

In September of 1882, Lizzie accompanied Robert as he drove sheep to his ranch in Hunt County. On the trip she became very ill, dying of typhoid dysentery a few days after returning home. Lizzie worked hard in her 30 years of marriage, performing labors of love with pride knowing she made a substantial contribution to her family's well being. Her labors are well recorded. She raised seven sons and buried an infant daughter. She should have had an album quilt presented to her upon leaving Kentucky made by loved ones lest they not be forgotten. While possible, there is no proof, so I made her one. Originally I planned to write the names of the women of our family on the center rectangle of each block in the quilt I named *Remembrance* but decided instead to keep the front plain, in keeping with the fact Lizzie teased and frustrated me with not naming most of her quilts and that family members didn't write names on the back of the old photographs. One day, I will write the names on a label and attach it to the back of the quilt.

There are several reasons for making the quilt, my homage, my tribute to Lizzie. Leaving her home in Kentucky, friends and family could have easily made her an album quilt, which was a popular gift at the time. Lizzie missed her mother and sisters and once they joined her, she was very happy. Whenever Robert was away from home, she was lonely and especially so when he was gone during the Civil War. It was during the war, responsibilities of the family, farm, livestock, and crops fell to Lizzie with help only from young sons, and a family friend. Her time of grief over the loss of her little girl was the saddest time of her life. Her most eloquent writing occurred in times of great emotion, in a letter to Robert during the war, when she was truly content or reflecting on a memory, and when she was heartbroken. These are the times that call for a remembrance.

Lizzie's writings and her record of work are a gift, and *Remembrance* is my gift to Lizzie.

Betsy's great grandparents, Jeff and Florence Carpenter and family. Betsy's grandmother, Ethel is the little girl with blonde hair.

Pasted to one of the journal pages is a portion of a letter to Robert from Lizzie written during the Civil War. *"I hope the time will come love – when this cruel war is won – that you can hasten home love – and be gone from us no more – and our lives will in peace together glide on life's stream and may nought disturb our pleasure nor mar life's hallow dream and for this I will pray love and watch until you come. Oh Robert we do miss you – hasten home - dearest love."*

Lizzie corresponded often with friends in Kentucky. One name in particular recurs throughout the years, Irene Pierce, could she have been Lizzie's best friend? Letters were written to her brother, John, who remained in Kentucky after the rest of the family joined Lizzie and Robert in Texas and to other friends there over the years.

From Lizzie's Journals

1863

February 22   I am lonesome for the one I love is far away and I can't be otherwise

1866

October 28   It has been almost two months since I have written any on thy fair pages dear journal – I have sadly neglected thee – But I can hardly say neglected either for sickness in a great measure has prevented me from writing, tis true I might have written sooner – or before this time but I have been busied, with other matters to the neglect of this – another little responsibility added to our family in the shape of a little blue eyed baby boy (Bobbie) So I fear dear journal you will be neglected more than ever though I will try to do my duty to both thee and my baby … I have almost all my winter sewing to do yet, but am hiring all the weaving do so I can do the sewing – ought to write Mrs Tipton this evening

November 6   I shall not say much to day and also ought to write a letter to friend Irene Pearce

1867

May 20 In the evening it blew up a rain and large hail – Our little boy Jeff Davis fell from the window up stairs down on a large rock lain in front just by the door – it hurt him very much indeed Drs Milson and Dye were here to see him – his head is badly swollen and I would not be surprised if his skull is fractured.

May 26 This past week I have done little work – Jeff is some better, but looks badly – I have only about 70 pounds of my wool picked – I must try to do better next week – little Jeff want me to do something so I will say Adieu

1870

December 18 Tis the anniversary of our Wedding – 19 years ago to day we were joined in holy wedlock … my mind runs back to that evening – so long ago – and it seems but yesterday – so vivid is the picture. It was all cold and snowy without, but warm and pleasant within and eyes full of love and cheeks full of health and lips of sweetness and words of of gaiety and where to day they are gone, some one way, some another and some are long since in their graves and some are scattered

1874

May 7 I am rather lonely – quilting by myself – Mr C gone away cattle hunting with Dick and Mat Clark *(the Clark boys were raised by Lizzie and Robert. They drove cattle to market in Kansas.)*

May 8 Mr C came back this evening – he is seldom gone from home that I miss him very much when he does go

1877

Finally a daughter for Lizzie, but poor Mary Katie born January 6 was never a healthy child. She lived only 14 months. During that time, Lizzie made far fewer garments and quilts, sent piecing out to a niece and apologized to her journal for not being able to care for the family the way she should.

1878

One month before Mary Katie's death, Lizzie wrote on February 10

Peaced on my quilt of nights – The Lovers Walk. *(Wish I knew which pattern she made as I can find no reference in my research.)*

The month after the babe's death, Lizzie finished piecing The Lovers Walk. That quilt is never mentioned again.

September 18 Our beloved brother Ben was taken to the spirit land last Sunday evening – I am trying to quilt on a quilt for the little bed – this evening I want to go see Mary Ann, oh I feel so sorry for her – she is in such distress

October 12 I am 46 years old to day – although the last year has been the most bitter of my life I have many things to be thankful for – we had a small gathering here yesterday as Gipson married Lula Bush – On Thursday we gave him a reception in the way of a dinner and a few friends and kinfolk to see him – we approve of his choice – think he has done very well and do hope and pray they may be happy in each others society – the past week I have been cooking and doing my housework – Lula has been helping me very much – batted some cotton and peaced some on a flannel quilt

October 28 I put in a quilt last week – one for Gipson – I got it about half done – Good shower this morning – caught plenty of water for this weeks wash

March 1876

March 6th Monday This morning is damp & windy

When Lizzie passed away on September 24, 1882, family and friends mourned their loss. Robert mourned for one year then married Nellie Tipton, a widow friend of Lizzie. Nellie and Robert would have one son Gano. For a year after her death, Robert continued to write in Lizzie's book. On those pages he tells of the crops and the weather, the boys and their wives and the happenings in their community of Plano. Robert wrote, October 6, 1882, "Dear Old Book – My Dear Wife has been buried 3 weeks today and how I do miss her no tongue can tell. There is not a minute passes when I am awake but what I think of her. The 12th of this month was her birthday, she would have been 50 years old – Rest in Jesus' arms dear one, your work is done."

Remembrance

Lizzie would have no doubt left her Kentucky home in 1852 with quilts to begin her new life Texas. The album block pattern featured here was a common pattern made as a gift for those leaving home so that friends and family would not be forgotten. I know from studying Lizzie's journals that her mother and sisters were also quiltmakers, and I am quite sure they would have made her a quilt for the journey. Lizzie was overjoyed when her mother and sisters joined her in Texas in December 1857.

Dear Lizzie, for all you wrote, in your record of work, your love of husband, family and friends, your faith, your quilts, accept this token, in remembrance.

Fabrics

4 ⅝ yards cream solid
1 ⅞ yards total assorted Turkey red prints
4 ½ yards for backing
⅝ yard red for binding

Cutting

From cream solid, cut:

24 – 1 ¾" x 4 ¼" rectangles (A)
48 – 1 ¾" x 1 ¾" squares (B)
72 – 3 ¼" x 3 ¼" squares – cut each twice on the diagonal (C)*
48 – 2 ¼" x 2 ¼" squares – cut each once on the diagonal (D)*
7 – 2 ¼" x width of fabric strips for the inner border
132 – 2 ⅝" x 2 ⅝" squares for the geese background
25 – 7 ¾" squares for the alternate blocks
8 – 5 ½" strips x width of fabric for the outer border

From assorted Turkey red prints, cut:

192 – 1 ¾" x 1 ¾" squares (E)
96 – 1 ¾" x 4 ¼" rectangles (F)
33 – 4 ¾" x 4 ¾" squares for the gees e border
8 – 2 ¼" strips x width of fabric for the binding

These triangles are cut oversized and will be trimmed after piecing.

Block Assembly

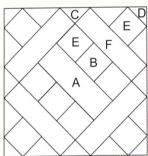

1. Sew 2 – 1 ¾" red squares (E) to either side of one 1 ¾" cream square (B). Press to the red. Make 2. Sew 1 cream rectangle (A) in between the 2 pieced units. Press to the rectangle.

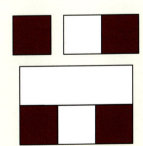

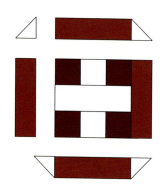

2. Add 2 red rectangles (F) to either side of the center unit. Press to the red rectangles. Next sew 4 cream triangles (C) to 2 red rectangles (F). Press to the red rectangles.

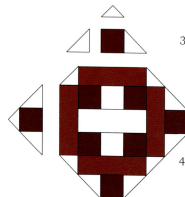

3. Sew 2 cream triangles (C) to one red square (E). Press to the red square then add triangle (D) on each corner. Make 4

4. Sew each corner unit to the sides of the center unit. Press unit to red rectangle. Make 24 blocks. Trim blocks to 7 ¾"

Assemble Quilt Top

1. Join 24 pieced blocks alternating with 25 – 7 ¾" cream squares as shown in quilt diagram on page 95. The quilt top should measure 51 ½".

Inner Border

1. From the inner border cream fabric, piece the strips to measure 51 ¼", make 2 and join to sides of quilt top.

2. Piece the remaining cream strips to measure 54 ¾", make 2 and join to top and bottom of quilt top.

Flying Geese Border

1. Make quick flying geese, four at a time from 4 – 2 ⅝" cream squares and 1 – 4 ¾" red square. Place 2 cream squares in opposite corners. Draw a diagonal line from corner to corner on cream squares as shown, stitching ¼" on each side of drawn line.

2. Cut apart on the drawn line. Press to the cream triangles.

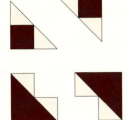

3. Place a cream square on each corner and draw a diagonal line on the cream square as shown. Stitch ¼" on each side of drawn line. Press to the cream triangles. You will have 4 geese units 1 ¾" x 3 ½" finished.

4. Sew 2 strips of 31 geese units and 2 strips of 35 geese units. Sew the strips of 31 to sides, then strips of 35 geese to top and bottom. The top measures 61 ¼" x 61 ¼".

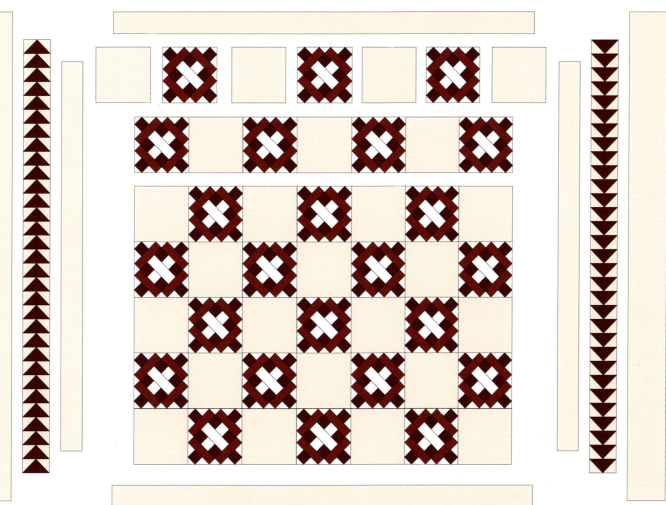

Assembly Diagram

Outer border

1. From the outer border cream strips, piece 2 strips to measure 61 ¾". Add strips to sides of the top. Press.

2. Piece the remaining cream strips to measure 71 ¾". Add to top and bottom. Press.

Finishing

Remembrance is custom quilted with feathered wreaths and a feather border. The quilt has a narrow 2 ¼" double fold binding in red.